Touching Greece

This is a work of fiction. Names, characters, places, and incidents are either the product of the author's imagination or are used fictitiously.
Any resemblance to actual persons, living or dead,
events, or locales is entirely coincidental.

Copyright © 2024 by Gordon G Hall

All rights reserved. No part of this book may be reproduced or used in any manner without written permission of the copyright owner except for the use of quotations in a book review.
For more information, e-mail: author@lakefell.com.

First paperback edition July 2024

ISBN 978-1-0686941-0-3

CONTENTS

PART	i
PART	ii
PART	v
PART	ix
PART	x
PART	xii

1	Foreword	1
2	Hello Kitty	4
3	Bear-faced	12
4	Mattress	18
5	The Lion of Amphipolis	23
6	Beached	24
7	Dylan	29
8	Reaping and Sowing	38
9	Springtime in Greece	42
10	The Road to Olympus	47
11	The Great AFM Quest	55

12	Euboea	62
13	This Land, This People	69
14	Imagination	71
15	Piraeus Lunch	77
16	Plus ça Change	81
17	The Man	86
18	Still Waiting	92
19	Greek Bathrooms	93
20	Greek Dentists	101
21	Greek Lifts	110
22	Greek Pavements	119
23	The Second Dog	122
24	Oxι Day	124
25	East or West?	125
26	Lazy Greeks	130
27	Nil Desperandum	135
28	Philhellenes	139
29	The Way Ahead	143
30	Without and Within	148
31	Take Heed	153
32	The Illusion of a Rebellion	156
33	Contrasts	159

| VIII | –

PART 168
PART 169
PART 171
PART 172

Touching Greece

Gordon G Hall

1

Foreword

I am an Englishman in Greece. What brought me here originally was a sense of challenge, to travel alone at the sort of age when most of my countrymen are toasting their slippers in front of a fire – or pruning their roses. I cannot say why I chose Greece. Perhaps it was a sense of solidarity in the face of Crisis, a vague idea that if I was going to spend my English pension anywhere then it might as well be in a country that needed it! But above all there is I think in the hearts of many Englishmen a feeling of affinity with Greece. Ancient Greece was part of our education, but there is also a sort of Byronic impulse towards this country.

As time went by I came to love the country. I started to write about my experiences. I began to record just a little of how I felt, and feel, about this land and its wonderful people. I tried to capture the strengths and exasperating little weaknesses with humour and with empathy. The result is a catholic collection of stories and articles. Some are serious, a few are satirical, others are self-deprecating, whilst yet others are just stories, usually based on fact. If I have offended anyone (other than the Germans!) it is unintentional and no doubt due to the overweening arrogance instilled into me by my birth and breeding.

In these articles and short stories I have carefully avoided getting serious over the devastating politico-economic issues that have beset Greece and her people over the past few years. It is in any case now a social crisis, caused largely by the shenanigans of the Troika. It is about these social issues that I have from time to time felt compelled to write. About half the pieces in this anthology are articles about the way that 'ordinary Greeks' have managed to cope with the Crisis. On one or two occasions (such as Barefaced) I have resorted to satire, but satire is not the most constructive form of writing.

Most of the other pieces are short stories that depict either the bumblings of an inexperienced old Englishman, or take a sideways look at various facets of the Greek way of living. There are a few 'real' short stories such as 'Mattress' or 'Reaping and Sowing', but these too are inspired by real events here in Greece.

The poems provide some punctuation. Three are sonnets, a form I find stimulating in that the restrictions of rhyme and metre add formality to the expression of ideas and emotions. *'Items from Athens'* was an experiment to see if it were possible to construct a valid poetic argument from three very mundane materials, whilst *'Take Heed'* is a bit of propagandist doggerel that was fun to write!

I would like to thank, wholeheartedly, the many Greek people who have been so kind to me and from whom I have 'stolen' the ideas for these stories. Their courage, optimism, and sense of enjoyment has been infectious, and I hope I have captured just a little of that in this small book.

2

Hello Kitty

The girl looked me in the eyes, desperately attempting to make out what it was that this old Englishman was asking of her.

I raised my voice slightly, and tried for the third time, "Thelo mia peseta" and then, attempting to throw a little light upon her incomprehension, "Gia tin paralia."

Clearly this was not working, which was disappointing. Travelling around Halkidiki on my own seemed to offer me the ideal opportunity to learn the language of the Greeks. So, with the merest smattering of linguistic ability aided and abetted by my Collins Greek Phrasebook, I was trying my best to speak in the tongue of this foreign but friendly land.

Any visiting Englishman who is attempting to say a few words in Greek is bound to encounter the problem of accentuation. His inability to grasp the need for correct application of this vital ingredient is bound to give rise to native amusement, incomprehension, and occasionally considerable embarrassment as a perfectly reasonable word, wrongly accentuated, can mutate into something rather more basic that had been intended.

Almost everyone in Greece, under the age of fifty, speaks some English, especially in the cities and holiday areas. So I had little doubt that the perplexed young lady who was patiently trying to decipher my needs did, in fact, speak English. I weakened, I gave in, I surrendered, "Towel," I said, "I need a towel for the beach".

It was as if a light had been switched on. "Yes of course," she said in almost perfect English, "this way." And she led me outside towards a rack of assorted beach-ware.

"Prospatho na milaw ellinika." I said, explaining why I was stumbling around in Greek rather than speaking to her in the English of which she so clearly had an excellent grasp.

"Good for you, not many visitors make the attempt."

I took this for high praise!

The shelf of beach towels was not offering me the kindest of choices. I could only suppose that the inhabitants of this fair land have an unnatural addiction to cartoon characters. The towels were masterpieces of Disney marketing but hardly suitable for a man, a man of my age, or indeed a man of my age who has a fairly substantial aversion to the close proximity of Mickey or Goofy.

Two days earlier I had enjoyed a long and very relaxing dip in the Aegean Sea and saw no reason not to attempt a repeat of the experience, alas without the company of my pleasant friend who had exhibited a total understanding of how to enjoy a Greek beach.

How different this experience had been to that of swimming off my much-loved Norfolk coast back in England. There the pebble beach provides an uncompromising barrier against the pounding North Sea waves, whilst the ever-shifting shingle indicates the strength of the side-current that had created this natural barrier through long-shore drift. Swimming there is a test of the hardy, or foolhardy, stripping off at the last moment to dash into the freezing, grey, sand-laden water, trying to judge the best moment to immerse oneself between the crashing waves. Five minutes of brisk exertion then an equally well-timed retreat to the much-needed warmth of a pair of trousers and a thick jumper. I recall that in my childhood my mother would hand out post-swim 'shivery bites' – pieces of chocolate that we kids would chew to stop our teeth from chattering! Such were summers in England.

Today I had checked out of my hotel in Panorama. Not you understand PanorAma, like the UK television programme, but PanORama. We may steal Greek words but we don't half muck about with their pronunciation! Anyway it had hitherto been simple enough to 'borrow' a hotel towel to take to the beach. Admittedly such an accoutrement was white, a little small, and smelt of lavender, but at least it was a towel. Signing out of the hotel had removed the slightest possibility of my utilising even this rather dubious object.

I drove the decent dual carriageway to Neo Moudania. I am not a great enthusiast of air-conditioning in cars and as the outside temperature, according to Mr Skoda, was just under 30 degrees I lowered my car window to enjoy the scent-laden air. I took the rather lesser route towards Sithonia, where the

Bougainvillea were stretching themselves in towards the centre of the road, making overtaking next to impossible, except of course for Greek drivers!

As I entered the township of Kalyves I spotted a small shop on the lefthand side of the road selling brightly coloured beach balls and parasols. I flung Mr Skoda to the right and onto the yellow dusty area of potholed wasteland that is this county's interpretation of the concept of the 'hard shoulder'. A blare of horn to my left indicated that I had failed to signal my intention to stop and had upset the driver of a large truck that was now disappearing into the distance. Clearly I was well on my way to becoming passably proficient as a Greek Driver! A nifty U-turn and a bumpy negotiation of some wayward concrete curbs left me mighty pleased that I was driving a hire car. And so here I was selecting my 'towel of the day' from an exceedingly unpromising collection of overprinted pieces of cloth.

I was feeling a bit stupid, dithering around whilst my friendly, English-speaking helper looked on with increasing wonder at the inability of this foreigner to make up his mind. I pushed Snoopy and Pooh Bear swiftly back into their rack and in desperation grabbed a towel from the bottom of the pile that seemed to be fairly plain and white with a bit of a pattern on it. Oh well, not too bad I supposed. As I placed my new purchase on the sales counter the girl looked at me with what seemed to me to be just the merest twitch of a smile playing around her lips.

"Five Euros", she said.

"Resta pente evro." said I, proffering a ten euro note and displaying, almost to the full my linguistic flexibility. I took the proffered change and, with a cheery "Effaristo," returned to Mr Skoda, bearing my brand-new acquisition.

I took my time in choosing exactly the right place on the beach. It was not over-crowded, but plenty of people had beaten me to it and had set themselves up, presumably for the day, lying upon plastic mats under sunshades. Perhaps my beach-craft was a little lacking in that I had neither of these essentials, however at least I had a towel. I chose a spot near a small group that seemed to comprise two youngish families and grandmother. To my right and a little further away lay a couple of deeply tanned young men who had recently emerged from the sea.

It seemed to be the proper form in these parts that one should lie on the sandy beach for a little while before venturing into the water and whilst this was hardly the way we do things in North Norfolk I did not wish to flout local custom. "When in Rome, do as the Romans do" seemed to be a curiously inappropriate phrase here in this country that had preceded the Roman Empire, and that had given that Italian state so much of its culture and heritage.

I removed my shirt shorts and sandals. I had taken the precaution of donning my swimming trunks in the hotel that morning, and was grateful for having had the foresight to do so. Although still wrapped in its packaging this new towel seemed a little small for covering anything other than the bare essentials! Well, seeing that I did not have one of those plastic mats. I would lie upon my towel. With a flourish I waved it open so that it settled upon the sand, a move that was beautifully executed so that the towel was lying fully unfolded and exposed.

An involuntary gasp left my lips and I took a pace to the rear. My discrete white towel with its modest pattern was hardly that! The white that had lured me into the purchase was revealed as the body of a cat, whilst the greater part of the towel was a shocking pink. The cat had a pink bow upon its fetchingly tilted head and a finger in its mouth, whilst all around it were multi-coloured little hearts floating around in a pink universe. At the top of the towel were the inviting words 'Hello Kitty'.

I flung myself upon this extraordinary object so as to shield it from the inquisitive gaze of my neighbours. The family seemed oblivious to what had arrived almost in their midst, although I rather think that Grandmother's right eyebrow twitched. However the two young Adonis' to my right had seen all! They were looking straight at me and shaking their heads. One seemed to be laughing. I chose not to look. I buried my head into Kitty's bow and shut my eyes.

Ten minutes passed. My back was starting to burn. I raised my head. All seemed quiet amongst my neighbouring beach lovers. With commendable speed I got to my feet, scrumpled Kitty into a loose ball, kicked my shorts over her to cover the few pink hearts still on view, and loped down to the sea.

I swam. I floated. I duck-dived. I cooled off. I enjoyed just drifting in this wonderful paradise of blue. I was as happy as a lone Englishman can be when he is living for the moment, and trying not to think about a dread impending future event.

The skin of my fingers wrinkled. I felt a twinge of cramp in my right calf. My thinning hair was not protecting the top of my head from the mid-day sun. It was time to face my fate. Reluctantly I emerged, staggering slightly, from the warm friendly embrace of the sea and headed for my scanty pile of belongings. Was it my imagination, or had the two young men moved a little closer to me?

I walked my final few steps up the beach, as would a condemned man. Doom was upon me. I reached down and with a fixed expression upon my face I whipped Kitty from under my shorts and wrapped her around my torso. The world continued to spin. No one seemed to be greatly interested. I mopped myself down a bit and with the air of a seasoned 'Hello Kitty' fan I spread the towel and once again lay upon it, this time on my back.

I dozed.

A shadow fell across my eyes. I opened them. One of my Adoni stood above me. "You are English," he said. It was not a question, more an accusation.

"Yes," I said, fumbling my way to my feet. He was a fine specimen of a very hairy gorilla, clearly the sort of man who pumps iron on a daily basis and has sufficient chest-covering to supply a very busy wig-maker.

In getting up I had of course fully exposed my Kitty.

"Hi, I'm Dimitris," he said, "Nice towel you have there." He was not looking at Kitty but running his eyes over my slightly paunchy white body in a somewhat discomforting manner. "My friend, Kostas, and I like it. It is funny! He does not speak English very well, but he understands . . ."

I hastily donned my shorts, dropping the towel to the sand.

Kostas joined us. He was a slightly less hairy gorilla, but a gorilla nevertheless. He picked Kitty up and flipped the sand off her before returning her to languish, fully exposed, upon the beach. The two of them smiled at each other. I swallowed. "I didn't mean to buy it."

They smiled at each other and at me. "It suits you," said Dimitris.

My imaginings of the sex-life of Greeks is a little limited, but I knew my Cavafy. How brazen was this pick-up?

"No, no, you have it all wrong!"

"Will you swim with us?" It was clear that Dimitris was the spokesperson, but Kostas reached out to take my arm.

"No!" I said, "Ochi", and then in a flash of inspired Greek, "Mou agapo gyneka."

My protestation that I preferred women to men rocked my new-found friends. It was, after all, a little unlikely that a lone man of a heterosexual disposition would equip himself with a pink Hello Kitty towel and lie upon a Greek beach.

I seized the moment, grabbing my shirt and slipping my feet into my sandals. For the last time I gathered up the towel,

"Here you are," I said.

As I fled I thrust Kitty into Kostas' welcoming embrace, "You keep her, I doubt whether she is really my style."

3

Bear-faced

They were, let's face it, scruffy. I knew that things would be bad, so was hardly surprised at the shaggy tattered coats or by how thin the bears were. What I had not expected was how they just seemed to accept their fate. There was no assertiveness, let alone aggression, just a listless kind of stupor that showed in the dullness of their eyes. They were existing, but hardly 'living' and appeared totally disinterested, indeed unaware, of the trickle of people that made their way passed the bars of their enclosure.

A fellow visitor, southern American I guessed by her drawl, was clearly distressed by their condition. "Oh, the poor darlings," she said, "they really are in the most terrible state."

A man, smartly dressed in lederhosen, turned to her "Good morning, ma'am, Wolfgang at your service". He all but clicked his heels. "I am the Inspector of Zoos. These bears had it too good a few years back, and now they are reaping the consequences. Quite right too in my opinion – and my opinion counts! Anyway, they are just bears what can they expect?"

"A decent life," replied the American, "such as they should have in a democratic country like my own. I guess these poor dears haven't seen a square meal in months, just look at the state of them. Those responsible should not be allowed to get away with it."

Whilst I had a good deal of sympathy with this trans-Atlantic viewpoint I think I would have walked on had not the Keeper who was accompanying the Inspector, joined the conversation, "Quite right, madam," he said, "but Thessaloniki Zoo is broke."

"How come?" I said.

"The financial people say that we have borrowed too much money against our real estate. Now we can't pay even the interest on this, so it's my animals that suffer – they go hungry."

"That's too bad," said the lady, "it is so unfair. It's not the bears' fault. They can't control what the zoo does. What is more they have a great deal of potential, they bring money into the zoo because of all the tourists that come here."

"I am told that visitor numbers have dropped right off over these last few years," I said. "Apparently there's no chance of the bears generating more funds, what this place needs is good solid investment.

"It should be run with precision. It needs a sound infrastructure, a proper business plan, and an imposition of austerity," said Wolfgang.

The Keeper responded, "But this place has just seen six years of austerity. Look at those bears, they just cannot take any more hardship."

I wondered if the zoo might manage to generate enough income for its survival. The Keeper said that he thought so, but at the moment all the money that they earned went to pay off the debt. Perhaps the debt could be written down? Wolfgang opined that this was not possible and wondered if the zoo was still fit to be a member of the Zoological Association of Europe.

"I thought the zoo had just appointed a new director," said I, "and I understand he has some radical new ideas? That sounds exactly what is needed?"

"Indeed," replied the Keeper, "and very popular Alexis is. But he can't convince the Association. He's been in discussion with them for over six months now. At first his colleague, Yanis, tried to explain in logical terms the economics of zoo-keeping, but the Members simply did not, or would not, understand him."

"I heard about that," said the American, "Their only interest was in perpetuating their bureaucracy, indeed they were affronted at this well-educated zoo director telling them what to do. The sheer temerity of it!"

"What happened then?" I asked.

"We had a vote," said the Keeper, "I'm none too sure what it was all about, but we were determined to keep the zoo independent. The vast majority here voted 'Όχι'. But what we said no to was never very clear!"

One of the bears slowly rose to its feet and ambled forward towards us. It was a pitiful sight, swaying slightly as it moved, drooling from its jaws. And yet from it emanated a very real dignity. It stopped short of the bars and with considerable effort rose on its two hind feet and looked squarely at us. Just for a moment its dull eyes sparkled as it fell back on all fours and turned to join its fellow. I think we all realized that there was a fire within it that had not yet been extinguished.

The Keeper was speaking again. "Yanis told his colleagues of a wonderful place, a sanctuary up in the mountains where bears thrive in their own ecosystem. He said it was sustained by goodwill and even had its own currency so that the Association had no say in the running of the place. He had run into terrible trouble with the Association because they simply would not entertain the idea of the bears leaving without paying their dues."

"Quite right too," said Wolfgang. "There should be no write-off. If these bears starve then it's entirely the fault of the zoo, years of mismanagement and no doubt rather more years of corruption in high places – now they want to have a free lunch! Bah!"

The American lady was not quite so sure. "Well, as I understand it, the Zoo was encouraged to mortgage its real estate. I know they have behaved rather irresponsibly, but my concern is the state of the animals. I mean surely you cannot condemn these bears to a lifetime of such a regime?"

"So, what's going to happen now?" I asked.

"Ah," said the Keeper, "You would hardly believe it. Alexis went back to the Association and told them the Zoo wanted to be treated more flexibly, however the Council immediately decreed that the zoo would get no further funds. Alexis tried to ration out the little we had, but you can see how the poor bears fared, just look at them."

"Grim," I said, "but surely Yanis' idea of the bear sanctuary was good?"

"Maybe," said the Keeper, "but we are unlikely to find out. The Association asked for his resignation as a condition of maintaining the zoo."

"So, what happened?"

"Nothing very much. The zoo was told that it could have just enough funds to pay the interest on what it had borrowed, and a few more scraps were made available for the bears. The Association decided that we must sell off parts of the zoo so that interest on the debts can be repaid."

I looked around me. The zoo had not changed despite the efforts of the new Director. The American lady's interest had been ephemeral. Once she had voiced her concern in a strident manner, she had simply wandered off. The lederhosen man seemed to be about to follow her.

"Are you off?" I said to him.

"Soon," said Wolfgang," I have inspected this zoo many times over the past decade or so. I think it would be better if it had decided to leave the Association, then we would have been able to concentrate on other, better, zoos. Now my colleagues and I will have to keep coming back here even more frequently to just check that the zoo is implementing the austerity regime that the Association agreed.

I turned to the Keeper. 'The bears don't seem to have done well under these new arrangements?"

"Not at all," he said, "indeed they are worse off now than before. The Director was forced to agree to all sorts of cutbacks, so we have less staff, fewer services, and rather more expensive food."

'What about the longer term? Will it work? Will the zoo prosper and become independent again?"

The keeper looked at me. He couldn't speak, but with a tear in his eye and a slight shake of his head he turned back to his beloved bears.

*

The real bears of Thessaloniki Zoo were transferred in the early summer of 2015 to the excellent bear sanctuary run so well by Αρκτούρος at Αετός near Florina. The 'mythical bears' are still on the verge of starvation. Alexis was replaced by a more hardline Director, without any discernable change to the situation. Wolfgang is no more.

4

Mattress

Anna closed her eyes and, in her semi-recumbent position, allowed the glossy catalogue to fall, open, upon her face. Just the smell of the new print was good, but even with her eyes tight shut she could still see the wonderful thing, the object of her desire, her insatiable desire, just waiting to be ordered – by her.

It had been a full two weeks since, with the help of her cleaning lady, she had wrestled the old mattress off her bed and left it leaning precariously against the wall so that its replacement could be laid straight onto the bed.. For the intervening days she had been sleeping in the spare bedroom on a single bed, suffering, as she liked to think, for her future comfort.

She was sorely tempted to go to the IKEA store on the outskirts of town to see this, the object of her passion, in the flesh so to speak. There she would be able to not just see it, but to touch it, to stroke it, to sit upon it and, if there were but few people around and she was feeling very daring, to lie upon it. But wonderful as the idea was she realised it would only be wasting time. Why prevaricate when she knew exactly what she wanted. The catalogue number was etched upon her memory. She roused herself from the sofa, opened her laptop and startled her debit card into disbursing a large sum to a certain Swedish company. Delivery would be the following day.

Anna did not sleep well. Her single mattress felt lumpy and inadequate. She tried to lull herself into a doze by imagining that she was lying upon her new one, but there was no mistaking reality. Never mind, tomorrow night she would sleep oh so well and all her troubles would fade away, soothed by glorious interior sprung technology. She would look out her very best linen sheets and pillowcases, nothing but the finest for this Queen of Mattresses.

All morning she fidgeted. Twice the doorbell rang, and twice it turned out to be leaflet distributors. 'Between nine and one o'clock' the store had promised. At five minutes past one she phoned them.

"Don't worry madam, our man is on his way, he just had a heavy workload this morning. I am sure he will be with you in half an hour."

Twenty minutes later the bell rang again.

"Yes, that's me," she said, "third floor."

She held her apartment door half open as the lift came to a stop at her level. A tall, rather scruffy, individual emerged, tugging at the large, obviously heavy, sausage that had shared the lift with him.

"This way, in here"

The sausage was well wrapped which was as well given that Scruffy was dragging it along the floor to, at her behest, the bedroom.

"It doesn't look very big," she said

"Don't worry luv, they roll 'em like this at the factory. Give it an hour or two and it'll be right."

She signed the delivery note that Scruffy held out for her. He headed for the door.

"Aren't you going to unpack it?" she said.

"Oh no, just delivery, that's what I do. You'll be right as rain with it Luv, just watch it don't flip on yer. Bye" And with that he was gone.

The dream had not unravelled, but it was fraying a bit at the edges. She was, as they say, petite, and hardly the person to be handling something as awkward and heavy as this. Also what had Scruffy meant by 'flip on yer'? Rather nervously she wrapped her arms around the upright cylinder of compressed springs and managed to ease it towards the edge of the bed.

"Just stay there," she said, and went off in search of scissors. The mattress stayed.

Better equipped she started to cut away very carefully first the polythene and then the brown wrapping paper. As she pulled the packaging towards the floor she could see the beauty of her new acquisition. It was everything she had dreamed of, a sort of creamy white with brown piping. "Oh you poor thing, you must feel dreadfully squashed, what have they done to you?" The mattress seemed to wobble slightly.

The compression was held in place by three thick dark straps that were secured by Velcro. She needed a plan of action. It might be possible, she thought, to undo the top and bottom straps then sort of half lean the beautiful thing over her bed whilst at the same time undoing the final, middle strap. With any luck it ought to fall open upon the bed, just needing a little minor adjustment to get it properly into place.

Anna, very gingerly, undid the top strap. The springs stirred slightly, but the mattress remained tightly rolled. Good, this was going to be easy. She stooped down and released the Velcro on the bottom strap. Again there was a slight stirring of springs, but as she started to straighten up there was a crack as the Velcro on the middle strap burst asunder. The springs, suddenly released from their compression whirled the mattress around, striking Anna. There was a chaotic moment of movement. Things were displaced, wrapping was hurled into the air, straps were re-joined, and the mattress did indeed flip, at least twice.

Early the following day Stelios and his mate Panos were on bin collection duties.

"Bloody mess here," said Stelios, "better give us a hand, it's heavy too."

"Load of old shit," said Panos. "mind you it looks almost new. It's like that time someone trashed an alligator, did I tell you about that,"

"More than once." Said Stelios giving the polythene wrapped brown paper bundle a disconsolate push with his foot. If a motorbike had not chosen to go by at just that moment he might, perhaps, have heard a slight groan. As it was the two men heaved the bundle into the dustcart and moved on to the next set of bins.

| 22 | – MATTRESS

In the apartment the old mattress had regained its rightful place. It lay serenely upon the bed. It was so content, so innocent, and so alone.

5

The Lion of Amphipolis

Ancient echo of Alexander's time,
tomb-guarder then of his warrior brave,
thence misplaced, and displaced by thoughtless crime
and so divided, lost in unmarked grave.
Until new strife brings you again to light,
awakening you from bi-millennial snooze,
exposing scattered remnants of your plight,
rudely unearthing the site of your abuse.

Restored afresh to leonine glory
sejant you pose eyeing your small domain,
statue smiling in memento mori,
repository of history arcane.

Guard still your bridge from Struma's southern shore
for all is by-passed save your mighty roar.

6

Beached

If it had been hot it would hardly be worth mentioning such. July in Halkidiki is supposed be hot, that is why we all love it so much. But today it was super-hot, the sort of day when you dare not look at the thermometer in case it registers 40 degrees, the sort of hot that makes grown men retreat from the beach and switch on the air-con in the car, the sort of hot where nothing moves – not even the sea. Except of course for the English!

Clad like a figure from the colonial past in white sun hat and safari jerkin, and allowing only the latter-day luxury of sandals, I parked the hire car in a convenient spot and headed for the beach. Whilst I was well aware of the lack of tide it seemed unwarranted that I should break the habit of a lifetime and leave my footwear at the edge of the water. Thus it was that I covered the final 20 meters at an unseemly pace saying "ouch" at every fleeting footstep as the sand seared the soles of my feet.

The sea was warm, but a delightfully cool warm compared to the air temperature. I wallowed. I was careful of my shoulders' exposure and the effect of the sun upon my, oh so slightly, balding head. This was not the normal dash and splash of those accustomed to the North Sea, this was how holidays in Greece should be, long and sensual and loving. My eventual retreat from the briny was only a trifle spoiled by a hectic leaping across the even hotter strand to the sanctuary of my sandals. But altogether it had been a thoroughly enjoyable experience.

I am not one to linger upon the sand. I do not 'sunbathe'. My fellow bathers had firmly retreated beneath large sunshades, the like of which I do not possess, nor indeed wish to possess. So gathering my towel I made my way with seemly haste to the car and its wonderful cooling system. Having knocked the sand from my footwear I switched the engine on and basked in the cold air emanating from the multi-vented fascia. This was a Good Day!

Reluctantly I accepted that I had to move on. I engaged first gear. Nothing happened. I switched the noisy air-con fan off, better to hear if the engine was running. It was, but the car was not moving. I tried reverse - to the same effect. Reluctantly I opened the door and, offering myself as a hostage to the painfully hot day, walked around the car. Three wheels were perched happily upon solid ground. The fourth, the nearside front, was digging itself into the sand in the general direction of Australia.

The situation required physical labour. I removed my safari jerkin. I knelt, exposed knees upon kiln-roasting sand, I dug with my bare hands, scrabbling at the loose sand. I tried the car again. Nothing moved. I left the car in gear and walked around to survey the situation. The wheel was gently rotating having dug itself far enough into the yielding substrate to ensure that the weight of the car was now borne by its front bumper, and that was resting its chin lovingly upon beautiful firm ground.

I needed help.

There was none immediately to hand save a couple of groups of mothers and kids. It was not female help that I required. I marched firmly in the direction of an unsuspecting male that was sitting innocently under a large sunshade.

"Parakalo," I ventured.

He looked around, clearly expecting further words from me.

"Milate Anglica?" I stumbled.

He shook his head.

"Autokinato stuck." I said, making pushing gestures.

He looked puzzled "Eleni!". A slightly plump and rather jolly looking woman came over. A few words were exchanged. She turned to me. "Kalimera, I speak some English. You need something?"

I explained, several times, my predicament. Eleni was calmly patient as I tried to get her to understand, remaining so as I spoke louder and louder, as is the wont of every Englishman when foreigners cannot understand them.

She spoke briefly to the man, turned and smiled at me. "This is my husband. He will help."

Husband and I set off across the silicon furnace. As soon as we reached the car he grasped the situation. He made 'stay there' signs and left in the direction of a large and expensive looking villa.

I dug with a stick.

I sweated profusely.

Five minutes later Husband reappeared carrying a long-handled spade and a catholic collection of sticks and planks.

He dug.

I continued to sweat.

Two more men appeared from the beach and disappeared into the villa. They reappeared. Our collection of assorted timber was enhanced. There was a lot of shaking of heads and the equivalent of "tut, tut" in Greek. There was much good-humoured encouragement of Husband to dig further or faster or both.

The taller of the two men beckoned me to the front of the car. "Pull" he said, making a crooked finger at me.

"I don't know," I said, "It's a hire car".

This clearly exceeded his grasp of English. He pointed to the right of the bumper. "Etho, Ne?"

I shrugged

"Ochi, Eki." He pointed to the left.

I shrugged again. Clearly this stupid Englishman did not understand about towing brackets.

Meanwhile the excavations had proceeded splendidly and timbers were being inserted under the errant wheel. There was a good deal of hammering of timber with timber until

Husband, clearly the leader of this scratch team, gave me a thumbs' up sign. I started the engine.

"Pame!" they all shouted.

And I went.

I stopped the car and got out to shake hands with my rescuers, but they were having none of it. "Filee mou," said Husband and, leaving the car in the middle of the sandy track, propelled me into his villa, followed by the rest of the crew.

A convivial half hour, turned into a convivial two hours. Tsipouro was consumed in considerable quantities so that I was rather less steady on my feet by the time I bid farewell to my new Greek friends.

I suppose I imposed upon them, but I left with the firm belief that they had welcomed the opportunity to rescue this stupid foreign visitor, not least because my predicament had in turn rescued them from the banality of beach-lounging with their families.

7

Dylan

Greece was on holiday! No, it was not summer, beaches and swimming, but it was a wonderful Spring day and the whole of Thessaloniki reeked of barbecue! Indeed it was because of this overpowering stench of charred meat that I had sought olfactory sanctuary on the Paralia.

I should have known about Τσικνοπέμπτη, but somehow this great day of carnival had escaped my attention. A compound word, Tsikno means 'the smell of grilled meat', and Pemte is Thursday. It is part of the Greek run-up to Lent when, in preparation for fasting Greeks like to make sure their bellies are well provided for. Actually, fasting in Greece is a wonderful culinary experience as you can enjoy the most gorgeous dishes prepared exclusively and especially to comply with the strictest Lenten abstinence!

So, there I was sitting on a large wooden bench on the Paralia and staring out into the bay where the coasters were lying at anchor awaiting their turn to be summoned into the port. Although it was, at least by my standards, a warm day, the perambulating population considered it still to be the depths of winter and was in no mood to shed its scarves or Puffa jackets.

Some of my fellow escapees from the bittersweet smell of barbecue were hurrying about their business whilst others strolled, arms linked, deep in animated conversation. Perhaps it was because I was daydreaming, or just that the sun was blinding me from the south, but I did not notice the rather gaunt young lady and her dog until they were almost upon me. The woman in question was well-dressed in a green outfit that would not have disgraced Robin Hood, thick green tunic, grey tights, and high-kicking fawn boots. Attached to her, at the end of a very long extendable lead, was a small white dog.

It may have been that these two, human and canine companions, had not been seeing eye to eye before they chanced upon this sedentary Englishman. I do not know, but whilst my comprehension of human behavior is somewhat limited, I pride myself upon having a keen understanding of the mind of Dog. It was easy for anyone to see that Dog did not want to walk at the speed that Human wished to attain. Indeed, Dog did not much want to walk at all. It was playing the game of 'let's stop and pee by this orange tree' and 'ooops, just a moment, I must have a scratch'. Human was not amused by such antics.

Then Dog espied the perfect 'delay'. Dog's eyes met mine for a split second, and a moment later it had jumped up on my bench and was sitting down next to me. Being at one with dogs I rubbed its back. Dog liked this and lay down on my bench next to me its right rear leg thumping up and down in harmony with my scratching.

Human was not amused. "Ella" she said. "Ella Dylan, TORA!" It is funny. I am no Greek speaker but have reached the stage in my limited linguistic ability where I can say a few words of the language and, usually, make myself understood. Indeed, I have less trouble than I used to in picking up the thread a conversation in Greek with my fellow humans. However, I have spent much of my life talking to dogs and find it nigh on impossible for me to communicate with them in anything other than English. I was a little daunted therefor when confronted by this small animal called Dylan that, despite its total refusal to come when called, was clearly a Greco-Canine communicator.

I smiled at Human and tried to look as if I was mildly embarrassed by this display of togetherness that had been foisted upon me. Under such circumstances we, the English, tend to apologies, even if we have nothing to apologise for.

"Lipamai," I said, exhibiting my apologies, but without much conviction.

I had however said enough for Human to grasp that Greek was not my native tongue. "Do you speak English," she said.

I admitted that to be the truth and to her further enquiry confirmed that I did indeed come from England.

"Westmorland Terrier," I said, "friendly little chap."

"He doesn't usually behave like this. He's been trouble all day, he keeps wanting to turn round and head back into town"

"Perhaps it's the smell, of meat" I said.

"Yes, and his stubbornness. Stupid dog."

"You call him Dylan."

"Yes, from the Magic Roundabout. That Dylan was pretty stupid as well. He's not really my dog, he belonged to my mother and we 'inherited' him a year ago. I don't really like dogs. I can't think why I keep him"

"At least you can pick a Westie up and carry him," I said. I was concerned that this anti-dog antagonism that his mistress was espousing would fall ill upon Dylan's ears.

"I might well have to. Dylan. Ella!" And so-saying she tugged so hard on the lead that my companion slid off our seat.

His remote ancestors might have hailed from Westmorland in the Lake District of England, but this was a Greek dog – and true to his kind he was not intending to exert himself any further. He sat down on the concrete walkway. The more that Human tugged the more that Dylan resisted. Human was clearly at the end of her tether.

The two of them struggled. Human had a weight advantage and was able to drag Dog along the Paralia just a few metres at a time, however the Westie was made of stern stuff. He sat his bottom on the ground and dug his front claws into whatever grip he could find in the rather slippery concrete surface. They progressed at an agonizingly slow pace. Eventually she waked back the few yards to where her animal was stubbornly squatting after having yielded no more than 10 yards, and picked up this refusenik of hers. Clearly she was anxious about something and wanted to get moving. Dylan was not anxious, well at least he was not keen to do anything more energetic than jump back onto my bench.

Caught by surprise Dylan did not stand a chance as he was hoisted into Human's imprisoning embrace. It appeared that he had met his Waterloo – and in a somewhat undignified manner. Human started off at a smart pace, but Dylan was not done yet. He employed 'strategy'. Even as the distance between us rapidly increased I could see that, as if accepting his status, he went limp, he appeared to give up. Human read these Westmorland signals, reckoned that she had done the trick, and dropped him gently onto his feet. Dylan hit the deck running and without pausing for a moment he hi-tailed it back towards me, trailing his lead and being pursued, hotly, by Human.

The situation was such that I failed to suppress a grin. It became a smile, and finally ended in a great gust of laughter. Dylan jumped up beside me. Human arrived rather more puffed and a couple of lengths to the rear, not at all pleased to witness my mirth.

"Blasted dog," she said, "he knows I'm in a hurry."

"Where are you going?" I asked.

"I promised to meet my daughter by the White Tower, and that was . . ." She looked at her watch " . . oh no, nearly half an hour ago."

It was Human that now had 'defeat' written large upon her features. Her mouth was open, her arms hung loose by her side, her whole body sagged. "Look," she said," I wonder if you would do me a great favour. I've got to get to my daughter right away.

Could you just hang onto Dylan for a few moments whilst I meet Eleni and make sure she's okay. I'll be back in ten minutes."

With hindsight I should have wondered if this Eleni possessed a mobile. It would have been the matter of a moment for her mother to have called her, but I am of an age that finds such gadgets useful but not exactly the stuff of everyday life. As it was Human patted the recumbent Dylan on his head, handed me his lead and took off.

"Won't be long," she said and before I could open my mouth to say "Οχι" she was fifty yards away going hell for leather in the direction of the town.

It was a surprise to me, although perhaps not to my more perceptive readers, that Dylan and I were still sitting in the same spot some thirty minutes later.

"Don't worry old chap, she'll be along soon"

Dylan wagged his stumpy little tail. Clearly he was both unconcerned about this turn of events and learning English fast.

I peered into the sunlight along the Paralia. The sky was of an untroubled blue, but a small dark cloud was starting to form in my mind. There was no sign of Human. Thirty minutes later remote possibility had hardened into certainty. I looked again at this small white bundle of independence.

"It's all your fault. You're stuck with me now."

After a further fifteen minutes cogitation I realized than in being 'stuck with him' I had come off slightly worse in the deal.

I got up from the bench and, good as gold, my new acquisition jumped down beside me and trotted along, contentedly at my heels. We passed the White Tower. Neither dog nor I paused for more than half a second. Human had long since passed this way.

"I suppose I have to feed you?"

He looked a bit mystified

"Food?" I said. All dogs wag their tails at the word, but clearly translation was in order.

"Thelis na fas?"

The dog looked at me.

"Lipon;" I said, "Do you want a meal you stupid mutt?"

At that Dylan came to life. His tail wagged and he did the doggy equivalent of a couple of barrel rolls.

I paid one Euro for a Koulouri. Dylan was not to be appeased by such. Perhaps we needed to find a butcher.

"I suppose you only eat meat."

If a dog can scowl, Dylan scowled.

Okay then "Mono kreas?"

The tail wagged. It had never struck me that I would learn Greek by talking to a dog.

But there was no need for a butcher. The smell of Τσικνοπέμπτη was even stronger than it had been earlier. We turned up Aristotelous and I slipped Dylan's lead. Without hesitating he made a beeline for the nearest barbecue. Oh, he knew how to play to the gallery! He sat up and begged, he did little somersaults, he even seemed to clap his front paws together. And he was duly rewarded. After about the sixth barbecue I reckoned it was time for a break. I sat on a low wall and Dylan, a rather plump Dylan with the look of a 'for now satiated dog' upon his face, jumped up beside me.

As a rather overweight Englishman wandering along the Paralia I had attracted scant attention from my fellow walkers. However, as a cheerful old Englishman with a charming little white dog sitting on a wall on Aristotelous I was feted. Young ladies whose Puffa jackets did little to hide their charms stopped and cooed over my companion. They stooped and cuddled this white bundle of canine complexes, and they talked to me! I tried to speak in Greek, but the questions came fast and furious. Yes, he was a Westie, no he was not from England, indeed his name was Dylan. The dog was, undeniably, happy at being the centre of such attention.

I became aware that amidst all the hubbub a rather pleasing dark haired, blue eyed, slim woman, perhaps in her early thirties, had been sitting on the other side of Dylan from me and had been gently stroking him.

"I lost my Westie just a couple of months ago," she said.

"I hate it when a dog dies, they are such good companions."

"No," she said, "I mean 'lost'. We were walking in the mountains of Halkidiki, one moment he was with me, and the next he was gone. My friend and I searched and searched but we just couldn't find him. I kept going back, week after week, but I will never know what happened to him."

"That's so sad," I said," and worrying because you just don't know."

"I keep saying I must get another dog, but I am not sure I have the time for a puppy."

The Great Idea had formed rapidly in my mind. I looked at the well-fed contented Dylan lying on the wall next to me, his paws in the air and having is tummy tickled by this dog-bereft stranger. It seemed like a pre-ordained act of charity.

"Look, "I said and, without perjuring myself to a vast extent, continued, "I have to leave for a month the UK within a week and I really don't know what to do with the little chap whilst I am gone. I don't suppose you would like to hav him would you?"

"Do you mean it?"

"Yes, of course I do. Tell me, what's your name?"

"Anna. Yours?"

"Gordon. Okay Anna, here's his lead. His name is Dylan. He is as stubborn as a mule and has just consumed six barbecues."

Anna nodded. "Okay. That sounds like a proper Westie"

"Dylan," I said, "Meet Anna, she's yours now."

He growled slightly

"'Anna." I said pointing at his new mistress.

The dog, his brief flirtation with the English language now a thing of the past, gazed into the adoring eyes of his new Greek owner.

"Bye," I said.

Both owner and owned glanced briefly at me.

"Yas sas," said the one.

And I swear the other winked at me.

8

Reaping and Sowing

With long-practised precision he turned the small tractor through 180 degrees, then engaged the plough as the machine started its return run. Nearly done now. It was a small well sheltered field, bounded by a series of rough hedges on three sides and his grove of peach trees on the fourth.

He was a smallish man, in that he was less than 160 cms tall, but his barrel of a chest and chunky upper arms suggested that he was not someone to be messed with. He had not been messed with. Never in his life until now.

The village was just under a kilometre distant. As a boy he had run truant through its narrow maze of streets, so confusing to a visitor, yet etched indelibly upon local memory. It possessed a charm, a spirit of historical continuity that had seeped into its walls in Ottoman days, even in places a distant memory of the Byzantine.

Unlike its ugly modern neighbour the place had not suffered greatly from the German occupation, nor from the ravages of the subsequent Civil War. Yes, atrocities had been committed. Not by foreigners, nor by factions fighting for the political future of their country. Here it was the villagers of the lynch mob who had torn apart the five 'collaborators' of the municipality. They had savagely enacted a terrible revenge upon those men of local substance who, by their efforts to placate the Occupier, had saved their village from the wrath of the Hun.

That was all a distant folk-memory now, and well before his own time. His father had been killed in 1949, his throat slit by a Nationalist. Now he had inherited these few fields from the grandfather who had taught him the ways of the land. Not that his duties as a farmer were unduly demanding. His mornings were spent in the καφενείο just off the village square. A dozen or so of them met at about ten o'clock every day. A game of cards or a couple of games of tavli kept him out of the house at the time of day when menfolk should not be within sight of the kitchen sink.

Then there was the lake. Only a river in his grandfather's time it was to here that he came almost every evening with his three rods, a practical source of food in these difficult times, but also, though he would have been loath to admit it, the fulfillment of his need to get away from home, to find some peace.

He was a local man, and always would be. There had been a time when he had left the village, just after his National Service, with ideas of seeing the world. He had got no further than Athens and had returned from those parts only a few months later with the woman who was to become his wife. His mother reacted as every village mother would have done.

Why not choose a nice girl from the village? Why bring in a stranger, a foreigner, someone who would always be alien to this close-knit community and its ways? But he was determined. Rather than be married in the capital, or even in the centre of his village he had chosen a small chapel in a village some 8 kilometers away up in the mountains. The marriage had not been wonderful.

They had laughed at him this morning in the καφενείο. What was he doing hitching up his plough at this time of year? Did he know nothing about farming? Had he forgotten everything his grandfather had taught him? He had let them chide him, simply replying that there was a time and a place for everything. They had let it go at that. He might not be a tall man, but he had never been worsted in a fight.

But there had been fights; verbal to start with. His wife had brought into the house her different ways; the ways of Athens. She cooked differently to his mother, she was lax about cleaning the house, about making the bed, about doing the washing up. Her dresses were colourful, and thin, and short. Her hair was sometimes blonde and sometimes red, rarely her natural dark brown. But above all she was dissatisfied. She moaned about the village life. She griped about his lack of ambition. She hankered after loud music. She missed her lively friends. She did not want a family. She talked constantly about leaving.

He had not borne this patiently. He was a man of the village, and he well knew that women needed to be kept in their place. A few well-struck blows about her body where they would not be on display to everyone. Later it did not matter.

Everyone in the village knew everyone else's business here, and there was not a man, or a woman either, who would judge harshly a husband who had to keep an erring wife in check. There was no question about allowing her to leave; the shame it would bring upon him would be unendurable.

He turned the tractor and started back up the field; the final furrow. The seedbed would not be harrowed for another three or four months, indeed he might have to plough again before he could rake it with the tines. But before he finished this last run there was still some planting to do. Deep planting.

He carefully replaced the spade behind the link bar of the tractor. There was more room there now that the bundle in the old carpet had been safely interred. Good nutritious stuff in that. It would give a fine start to anything growing there. He engaged gear and expertly ran the furrow out over the freshly dug ground. The disturbance caused by his digging was scarcely noticeable except to the trained eye.

He was not an imaginative man, but he wondered about the crop that might grow from this place in the coming summer. What young sweet shoots would push up from under that damned oblong of ground? Would the flowers be just a bit too colourful? Would they be of a species native to the village? Would their petals be blonde or even red? And would their leaves grow just that little bit too short?

9

Springtime in Greece

It would be tempting to suggest that the resumption of direct flights from the UK to Thessaloniki might be some form of official recognition of the end of winter, a harbinger of the heat to come. The changing of the season is certainly not a gradual or incremental process but a series of forward forays into the freedom of Summer and hasty retreats to the safety of Winter. It entices the eager to shed overcoats and boots, only to retaliate the following day with cold and rain.

This was a situation I had not fully appreciated before I disembarked from the warm but cramped aircraft at Thessaloniki and emerged into a biting north-easterly that threatened rain or worse. So this was April in Greece? Perhaps I should have been alerted earlier by the glorious view at 25,000ft from my starboard-side window of a snow-laden Mount Olympus, but the sight had been so dramatic that I just reveled innocently at the grandeur of the scene before falling into to wondering whether the Olympian Nymphs were, at this time of the year, inclined to disport themselves in ski pants whilst cavorting in the snow fields of the Perivoli.

On the airport bus it was easy to distinguish homecoming Greeks wearing their thick coats or Puffa jackets from the transient Brits dressed in light trousers and sun hats. I had at least resisted an almost overwhelming desire to don a pair of shorts, but more because of the scant protection they would have offered to my white knees at 5am in Manchester airport than to a serious understanding of the vagaries of springtime Greece. Fortunately, or more accurately as a result of the inadequate airline baggage allowance, the excess of clothes that I was wearing made up in the quantity of their layers for the paucity of their protective qualities.

Meeting me in the arrivals hall Hara had no such problem. Winter, to her mind, was still firmly established and she greeted me wrapped in a fleece that would not have disgraced a small polar bear and boots that looked as if they might have high-kicked themselves all the way from Texas.

The main road towards Halkidiki was easy driving and Hara's small car made good time. There was very little traffic on this normally busy highway to the most popular seaside holiday destination in northern Greece. "I suppose all the visitors must have arrived on Saturday?" I hazarded.

"What visitors, when do you think the season starts?"

I lapsed into a contemplative silence.

Half an hour later Hara turned off the main road and took the shore-side route in the direction of Kalyves, her small car happily negotiating the ridges of blown sand and carving its way through the fallen pinecones. We came to a flooded area.

I could just make out the muddy looking bottom of this small inland lake that had once been the beach road

"Best go back," I said. "I'm not sure you can make it through here. It's pretty deep."

An astonished glance, selection of first gear, and a liberally applied accelerator and we were through.

"Greek road," she said.

"I thought they would have cleared the place up before the start of the season, but it is still an awful mess."

"They will."

I wondered if her understanding of English was a bit deficient in relation to the use of tenses. I said nothing, but noted with concern, rising to alarm, that the bars and Taverna along the beach were firmly closed.

Hara's apartment was right on the beach, but already the sun was slipping down leaving just the very peaks of Olympus outlined against in its golden rays, and I was hungry. It was a pity, for every Englishman wants to head for the beach as soon as he is within striking distance of sand and sea, but sadly I had to restrain myself. It was time to eat.

"Not much open," I said, "is it early closing day or something?"

Hara looked at me a little oddly. "Come on, bring your jacket, and I'll drive you to the best fish Taverna in town." So saying she picked up her small polar bear and led me outside. It was already cool enough to warrant the wearing of a light sweater. Just a short drive and in a few minutes we were sitting at an outside table with the sea lapping in a fond manner almost at our feet.

Hara ordered for both of us, and as water then Greek Salad, then wine, Octopus, and Shrimps were placed before us we chatted away. The blue waters beside us turned dark and just a little threatening whilst the hitherto gentle breeze from the northeast began to gain in strength that which it lost in warmth.

The meal was indeed excellent and the red country wine rough but undemanding on the palette. The wind curled around the side of the taverna, stronger than ever and cutting at my back, insistent and decidedly cool. Hara donned her fleece. She looked cuddly, happy, and warm.

"Best put your jacket on," she said, "it's getting quite chilly. I'll go and get it from the car. You wait here."

"No, no, no. I didn't bother to bring it. I'll be fine, it's just wonderful sitting here."

"That was very stupid."

Greeks do not mess about with platitudes, nor do they eat very fast, liking to take their time over a meal, two or three hours being par for the course. Thus it was that by eleven o'clock we were still lingering by the now wintery shore whilst my back progressed from somewhat cool, to downright freezing. Finally the nerve endings gave up hope of survival and relieved me of all feeling. I was numb with cold. Eventually we finished what was indeed a lovely meal. I staggered slightly as I tried to get to my feet.

"You OK? You must be cold."

"No, hardly at all," I said trying to repress the chattering of my teeth, "just a tiny bit on the cool side."

It is unusual for me to sleep in, but it was nine o'clock the next morning before the sun streaming in from the balcony window awoke me, inviting me to come out and play. I donned my swimming trunks flung a towel in what I hoped was a rather rakish manner over my shoulder, tripped lightly downstairs and flung open the French windows better to savour the scene prior to skipping across the beach. Rather hastily I shut them again.

"What on earth are you up to?" said Hara from the kitchen.

"Just an early morning dip." I replied, "but perhaps it's a little too soon for this time of year, best let the sun get up to warm the land."

"Do you know what the time is?"

I consulted the kitchen clock. "Eleven o'clock, it must be wrong, my watch says nine."

"I think you must still be on UK time." Hara, wearing a thick dressing gown and warm slippers sat me down on the sofa gently prizing the towel from my grasp and draping it as a warming shawl over my bare shoulders. "Look, this is Halkidiki. It is late April. No one swims here before the end of May. Don't be silly. Go have a warm shower!"

My dreams of Greece in the springtime were rapidly fading as I stared longingly out the bathroom window across the beguilingly bright blue Aegean Sea. It might have been the sound of distant thunder from the North, but more likely it was the laughter of the Gods on the far-off snow-capped Olympus as Zeus regarded the antics of this misguided Englishman.

10

The Road to Olympus

"Go to Dion," she had said, but that was several hours ago, as I was leaving Pella. In any case she hadn't actually said it but sent me a text message to that effect. I tried to argue that I did not need to see another seat of ancient Macedonian power, and that what with Pella and Virgina a visit to this Dion place seemed a bit excessive. However my far-away guide was unyielding and the text was unambiguous as to where I should go. It was however more than a little light on the navigational front. I had very few clues as to how to find the place.

Driving around the lesser roads of northern Greece can be a trifle challenging to an old Brit even in the best of circumstances. However not only was I on my own but my map of Northern Greece seemed to be under the impression that anything south of Katerini was part of the Peloponnese! Nevertheless fortune smiled on me, if a little weakly, in the form of my iPhone and its ubiquitous Google Maps. Or at least it was able to do service if I removed my sunglasses and screwed in my monocle. Such a procedure is not to be recommended whilst actually driving.

I set of to the South.

One hour later found me floundering around somewhere to the east of Katerini making futile attempts to persuade Mr. Skoda to find his way to the west of the National Road. What is more both he and I were thirsty, very thirsty. Quite why we were where we were was a bit of a puzzle to me, but here I was in some wonderful agricultural country, bowling along single-track roads without even a farm tractor to impede my progress, or offer me directions.

Mr. Skoda had been telling me for some time, by means of a very insistent winking light on his dashboard, that if he did not quench his overweening desire for petrol very shortly then he and I were going no further together. I knew how he felt, for I needed liquid myself – I was desperate for water. The temperature gauge informed me that it was 36 degrees. The sky contained not one solitary puffy white cloud. It was hot. I was thirsty.

I turned another right-angled corner. The road stretched out ahead of me, shimmering slightly with the heat haze. The fields looked parched. Nothing was moving except me – and, very slowly, Mr. Skoda!

It took two minutes to reach the next right-angled bend. I turned south, towards the sun and replaced the dark glasses that I had removed in a vain attempt to locate my position by means of the iPhone.

Ahead there was what must surely have been a mirage! In the middle of nowhere, sticking out of the dusty desert there was a dwelling, and more than a dwelling for standing slightly forlornly in front of the house were two, rather ancient looking, petrol pumps. I slowed even further, then burning up what must have been the final drops of fuel I pulled up at the pumps. A man was sitting in the shade of an enormous parasol with a bottle in front of him. A little reluctantly he raised himself from a decrepit lounger and made his way over to me.

"Peninda evros, parakalo". He nodded, apparently my rudimentary Greek was sufficient to accomplish this transaction. But I needed more. I eased my sweaty body from the car and walked around to where he was holding the nozzle.

"Nero?" I asked. He looked a little blank. 'Water" I said in my mother tongue. The man shook his head, clearly even less a linguist than I. I made drinking signs and said "Nero" again rather louder, remembering to stress the final 'O' rather that pronounce the name of a Roman emperor. The man shook his head.

I gave him the fifty euros for the petrol and was turning to go when he caught me by the arm "Apo pou isai?" he asked.

"Eimai apo tin Anglia." I was more than a little proud of being able to say in what I hoped was passable Greek, that I hailed from England. He gestured for me to stay and disappeared through the steel door of a concrete bunker, emerging a moment later with a huge bottle of water. He handed it to me. It was wonderfully cold. I fished in my pocket for a couple of euros but he was having none of it, instead he grasped my arm a second time and ushered me over to his parasol.

"Oi Angloi einai filoi mou", he said. Good, so he liked the English. He sat me down and poured liquid from his unlabelled bottle into a battered old cup that he handed to me, helping his own glass at the same time to another of the same. "Yasas," he said, clinking drinking vessels with me.

There followed one of those strange conversations that occur only occasionally between men that have something in common but hardly speak a word of each other's language. By gesture and mime I gathered that something had happened in the last war that had endeared his village, and what I think were his parents, to the English military. I knew that the English had helped the partisans from time to time, and I think that this is what he was telling me. In any case fifteen minutes later and a further mug of whatever the drink was and we were the best of friends. Reluctantly I parted company with this Friend of the English having obtained from him a vague idea of how I make my way to Dion.

I did not like Dion. This may have been in no small measure due to its museums and archaeological sites closing at 3pm sharp on Fridays. It was also a place of tourist gee-gaws and so-called taverna offering steak and chips. This was no place for a neo-philhellene! I regained the peace and calm of Mr. Skoda and decided that we ought perhaps amuse ourselves by following a sign that said 'Mt. Olympus'.

Ahead of me the Olympian bulk rose impressive, burdened as it is with the classical mythology taught to successive generations of school children throughout the Western world. Its flanks were clothed in a coat of green as trees and shrubs fought to maintain the honour of sheltering the resident Nymphs.

The road became interesting throwing tighter and tighter hairpins in an attempt to impede my progress, however the feisty little hire car was game for this. Eventually we came to a small open space area where a couple of cars were parked. From this the road turned to a dirt track, but there was a large sign next to this inviting route saying "Mount Olympus – Open'. No doubt fortified by the two mugs of some uncertain alcoholic beverage consumed an hour or so back with my English-loving friend I needed no second bidding.

This however was not a teasing gentle un-macadamed track such as is found in much of Greece. This was the Real Thing. It was steep, it was rough, and it was very narrow. As I progressed I wondered, far from idly, what would happen if I were to meet another vehicle coming in the opposite direction. These fears were groundless. There were no other vehicles. Just occasionally there would be 50 metres or so of concrete road where storm water running down the steep ravines had washed out the gravel, but I was soon back on the rutted stony track. And Mr. Skoda and I were entirely on our own.

I cannot say how far I went, but it was a very long way – but then Olympus is a very large mountain. I began to become just a little concerned. There was no one anywhere nearby. My car, although it was a plucky little thing, was hardly up to the task. I was far from sure that I was up to the task! How long could I keep going before either Mr. Skoda had a puncture or I lost concentration? The consequences were the same in either case – and it was a very very long drop! I was looking desperately for somewhere where I could turn. But there was no such place. I tried in one spot, but as I backed towards that sheer 1,000 metres as part of a multi-point turn my nerve gave out, so car and I continued our ascent.

Some 15 minutes of this does not seem long when one is happily bowling along a smooth motorway. It is a lifetime on Olympus! At last I found a place where a wash-out had provided just enough space to turn the car. I backed, oh so carefully towards the void, then forwards no more than a metre towards the wicked little drainage ditch that ran along the vertical rock-face. If I dropped into that I would never get out. I shuffled the car back and forth until I was facing downhill and let out a great sigh of relief.

It was short-lived, for the descent was far more dangerous than the climb due to the insubstantial road surface and almost total lack of grip. Poor Mr. Skoda did his best as he slithered his way down the gravel track. I tried cadence braking. Pathways on Olympus have not heard of cadence braking. I went as slow as I could, but all the same I was only half in control of the car. The Fates had decreed that Zeus was in charge. Every time I came to another hairpin bend I released the brakes to regain some steering, but that meant I was going much too fast as I exited each corner. Slither, corner coming, release brakes, gather speed, steer, more speed, straighten wheel, slither and slide trying to brake . . . it went on and on and on. At last I regained the small car park with an overwhelming desire to relieve myself!

I looked carefully at the 'Olympus Open' sign that I fancied had nearly killed me. There must be something wrong with it? My Greek is not very good, but with the help of my trusty Collins Greek Dictionary I deciphered the wording. Apparently my 'road' was a walkers' track, and that which was 'open' was a mountain refuge.

Items from Athens

An attempt to create some meaning from three mundane items found, by chance, in Athens, a Candle Stub, a Metro Ticket, and the National Flag

Flickering disconnection.
Candle casting cut-off
shadows
of waxen poverty.
Poor substitute
for poor people.
Hands it will not warm,
hearts it cannot gladden,
eyes that turn in desolation from
such guttering despair.
We who gave democracy
have nothing left to give.
From Monastriki,
commercial hustle, to
Agios Demitrios,
desperate bustle.
Metro stations heading south,
life-line heading down.
Ενα ευρω σαραντα is all it takes

and takes and takes and takes.
Ενα ευρω σαραντα the demand
to ride, to slide, from prosperity to
the end of the line.
And it strikes home,
as workers strike,
and strike and strike again
Konstantinos Koukidis
is still alive
in Greek hearts,
flagged up for our country,
hero for posterity.
So wrapped in our own blue and white
we all must jump,
jump now,
to our destiny,
rather than surrender,
surrender our souls.
Fight Merkel jackboot,
fight Troika bonds,
fight Papandreou legacy.
We heroes aspiring to be Greeks, fight
our fathers' foe with changed weapons
for changing times. So
Burn the Candle.
Validate the ticket.
Fly the Flag.
Ελευθερώνω Ελλάδα !

11

The Great AFM Quest

He is large or, to be more accurate, he is fat. His necktie hangs loose around his unbuttoned collar. It is conceivable that, long ago, button might have reached buttonhole. If such a result could ever have been achieved it certainly is not the case now. An unlit cigarette hangs precariously from the man's lower lip as he growls a torrent of words that fall harshly upon my English ears. Was it a mistake to come to this police station? It is certainly less than wise for us to have entered the building and thereby exposed ourselves to this protector of the Greek state.

In Greece there is only one way for a foreigner, albeit one from a European Union country, to approach the gaining of a kind of national insurance certificate, an AFM – pronounced aff-eee –meee, that being to treat the whole process as an amusement, a sort of slow-moving farce. Stay in the country for a short holiday and you may well not encounter the wonderful bureaucracy that slows this already relaxed country from gentle inaction to a pace that would not disgrace a slug.

Couple this with a complexity that would baffle a chess Grand Master and you have the Greek System.

What I want to do is to buy a used car. This is something that most people will have done in the UK, where it is an easy enough matter. All you need is to place a large cheque in the seller's hand in return for the keys. Sending a simple slip of paper to the licensing authority in Swansea completes the transaction. But this is Greece!

Besides the need to treat everything as a somewhat overlong form of amusement you will, unless you are a proficient linguist, require a native Greek-speaker – and best that you choose one from the immediate locality. If you have a lawyer friend in Larissa do not set him or her upon your quest for an AFM in Thessaloniki. The guidebooks will tell you that, with the exception of Crete, there are no regional accents in Greece. Do not believe the guidebooks!

So having chosen a pleasant sunny day when I feel both relaxed and in need of some light entertainment, I equip myself with humour and my Greek friend, Hara, and sally forth in her car to have an afternoon of jollity and form-filling amidst the labyrinth of Greek officialdom.

"You drive, Gordon, you need the practice."

"So where first?" I say.

"We will go to the KEP, take the main road. Follow that van – no not so close. Mind the pedestrian." I am being treated as if I am a learner driver. "Turn left NOW. Ochi – sta dexia! Gordon, what are you doing?"

"You said 'turn left'."

"Well I meant right.

"How am I supposed to know that?"

Don't be silly, Gordon. Now turn round."

Changing the subject seems the best way to keep the peace. "What is a KEP?"

Hara explains that it is a Public Service Centre - a sort of clearing-house for local authority matters.

Surprisingly the place is almost empty although the lines of lonely-looking empty chairs suggest that this is unusual. A man, presumably the Manager, is on the point of leaving. Well it is just after mid-day and he has no doubt been at work for more than an hour. His two assistants remain, possibly intending to stay for a further half hour before shutting up shop. The rather more doe-eyed of these paragons of the people, runs a comb through her hair, pouts at her colleague, and blows a kiss to a passing boyfriend before beckoning us forward.

At Hara's side I adopt a pose of casual indifference such as might best befit a foreigner who does not want to appear too interested in the minutiae of legal matters. I attempt nevertheless to appear as if I understand every word of the conversation. However the dialogue swoops and soars without the need for either help or hindrance from me.

Greeks can talk. And I don't mean that they can say a few words. In fact I doubt if the concept of 'few words' has ever entered the Hellenic consciousness. No they talk earnestly, and perhaps just a shade aggressively to English ears, non-stop hardly pausing for breath for hours on end. They also have an uncanny ability to speak and listen at the same time, thus conversation really is a non-stop two-way thing with each party gabbling on at the other whilst picking up the gist of simultaneous incoming words. This tends to obscure the process of question and answer and continues until both participants are exhausted. Oddly to my mind this moment occurs to both protagonists at exactly the same instant. There is silence. Hara turns to go.

"Effaristo!" I say in my best Greek accent. Either such a nicety is superfluous to the situation or my best Greek accent lacks a certain something. Doe-eyes ignores me whilst Hara whisks me firmly out the door.

"I thought we were going to fill in some forms?" I say, fumbling passport, birth certificate and last year's tax return back into my trouser pocket

"We have to go to the Immigration Office," she says.

"But I'm not an immigrant! The UK is a fully paid-up member of the EU and there are all sorts of treaties about mobility of labour and the like."

"Gordon, you have to understand me, this is Greece! Anyway the immigration office will be closed by now. Lipone, we will go to the Police Station."

For reasons that are far from compelling the local police station in Greece is a further bastion of this country's bureaucracy. It would seem that if you require a passport, an ID card, or a Residency Permit it is to the local cop shop that you should turn your footsteps. I try to explain to Hara that this is not how things work in the UK, that policeman in Britain prevent crime and catch criminals and do not involve themselves in civil matters. She seems surprised and not very impressed.

We drive through the northern outskirts of the city. I approach a multi lane junction. The traffic lights are not working. I proceed with caution. I halt, looking left and right. Behind me a car horn blasts, then another joins in. I am holding up a string of cars. I start off across the road.

"Look out! What are you doing Gordon, trying to kill us?"

"Don't your traffic lights work in Greece?"

"You have to watch out, especially for motor bikes."

"What about the Highway Code?"

Hara looks at me a little oddly. I can only assume that the Greek Highway Code is not high on the bestseller list of this country.

The police station is just an end-of-terrace building on a street corner, however its appearance is not far removed from the barbed-wire encampments of the Ulster Constabulary at the height of the Troubles. Hara approaches a young uniformed officer who is ensconced in his over-size sentry box. His words of welcome, if they are such, compete with barked messages on a radio strapped to his shoulder. He waves his hand towards the main door. Things seem to be going well. We have gained consent to enter this fortress.

Inside all is chaos. Police everywhere, donning flak jackets and strapping pistols to their waists. What can possibly be afoot? Perhaps there has been a terrorist attack, a school shooting, or is there a mass murderer on the loose? We are shouted at. I do not understand. Hara clutches my arm protectively as, stopping barely short of serious physical force, we are summarily ejected from the building. Any conversation will now have to take place on the doorstep.

"What's happening?" I ask

"Some sort of urgent Criminal Investigation is going on." Says Eirine, "It's very confidential so they are chucking the public out of the place."

I contemplate with glee that this emergency might involve the anti-corruption squad arresting a senior politician. But the rich and the powerful in Greece protect themselves well from any such exemplary measures.

Thus it is that on this sunny afternoon we are facing a flabby-looking, scruffily dressed and totally disinterested policeman. I again adopt my attitude of slightly haughty indifference reasoning that such a pose might strike some distant chord of discipline into the man. However he seems totally unaware of my presence. His gaze is firmly fixed upon Hara but not upon her eyes. This time it is a one-way conversation punctuated by the occasional pause as the man shifts the still unlit fag from one side of his mouth to the other. Then suddenly it is over, for him Hara has ceased to exist. He turns in an equally disinterested manner towards the next person in the queue.

"Not good?" I say.

"He says you do not have to have an AFM."

"But the garage people won't sell me a car unless I produce one."

Hara shrugs. "This is Greece," she says. "Come on, that's enough for one day. Let's go and find ourselves a coffee."

Clearly such entertainment is to be savoured, not hurried but sipped as slowly as the Greek coffee that now sits before me. Perhaps tomorrow, or next week, or the one after that we will tackle the Immigration Office, or the Tax Office, or some other wonderful Greek institution. In the meantime my car-to-be awaits me.

12

Euboea

The road climbs its way up the hillside and into the lush green of the forest. This is better than my recent encounter with the grim modern highway from Eleftherios Venizelos airport to Chalkidis. Mind you to my relief Fotini drove that section after meeting the plane from Manchester.

"I'm going to take you to a very special place," she says.

"Where's that?"

"It's a spot I used to visit quite often when I lived in Athens, I haven't been there for a simply ages."

We have crossed to the island and I have taken over the driving. Now the coast road is behind us I am enjoying this narrow twisting road in the interior of Evia.

"Where are we going, is it in the mountains?"

"Just this side. It's a tiny little chapel, built into the rock. It's so gorgeous, and there's a great little taverna there where we can get something to eat."

"Good. I mean about the chapel; I've never been to an Orthodox church before. But also good about the taverna, I haven't eaten anything since Manchester, where at five o'clock this morning I encountered a floppy pastry thing that might have once aspired to croissant-hood."

I am more or less managing the switch to driving on the right. It is easy with a left-hand drive car and in Greece a little idiosyncrasy in one's driving is not just accepted; it is positively welcomed.

"I think I've got the hang of it." I say as we rather recklessly negotiate a road junction that suddenly leaps out at me, "just can't make out who has priority at cross roads."

"Is it very different from this in the UK?"

"Hell yes," I say, "we have a compunction to regulate everything. At a junction like that you would get a warning sign about 100 metres in advance. This would be followed by priority signs, road marking, the works."

She pats his hand in a friendly way. "Ah well, this is different, this is Greece."

Fotini speaks excellent English but with the attractive slightly guttural and 'r' –rolling accent of most Greeks. I concentrate, as best I can, upon driving. Fotini is a competent navigator.

"It's just down here, be careful, the road is narrow."

We are heading downhill into a tree-lined gorge. "Oh, I can see it now, what a wonderful place".

I take my eyes off the road to look at the grotto-like scene and as a result have to swerve the car rather sharply into a parking spot. It is probably just as well that there are only a couple of other cars here.

Out in the fresh, hot air I breathe in the beauty of this place. In front of us a large river dashes itself down the rocky chasm with a splashing rumble of sound. Trees line both banks and there is a small concrete bridge over the torrent. Fotini takes my hand in hers and leads me over this to a small sandy-coloured building on the other side.

"So this is your chapel." I say, pausing to take in the scene.

"It's very small and very wonderful. Are you coming in?"

It is dark inside and even though I take off my sunglasses it still takes a while for my eyes to adjust to the dim light provided only by candles. The place is very small, with icons on the walls and at one end a small gated off section with a table and a cross. It is a place of much feeling. Although it is a peaceful and loving sanctuary now. I fear that dark things have happened here in the past. I am not sure I want to know about the details. It is all too easy for a blundering Englishman to make false assumptions about the recent history of these mountainous parts of Greece.

Ahead of us there is a small tray of candles. Fotini takes several of these, plants them in the soft sand of the tray and lights them.

"What are they for?" I ask

"My friends and relatives who are in trouble or who have passed away."

I take a candle from the stack over on my left. "Should I light one?"

She places hers with those candles she has already lit. I place mine a small way apart, not wishing to trespass upon her thoughts for her family. She looks searchingly at me, picks her candle up and moves it next to mine. As she does so her hand searches for mine and gives it a squeeze.

"Should I give something for the candles?"

"Just a few cents will do."

I put a Euro in the box. To my right there is a rock pool that leads under the chapel wall. There are coins in it. I make to throw some money in, but Fotini catches my arm before I do so, "You should make a wish."

"We both will." I put a 50c coin in her hand. Together we throw our coins into the still, green pool. I turn to her, "What did you wish for?"

"If I tell you it won't come true. So don't tell me yours either."

We emerge into the bright sunlight. I have not said a great deal to her about how pleased I am that she brought me here. I am just, rather selfishly and quietly, soaking up the whole of this experience.

"Well," she says, "I don't know if you like the place, but I guess we had better do something about feeding you?"

"This is an incredible spot and I love your chapel. Thank you so much for bringing me here, it was a great idea of yours."

There is no one else sitting at the outside tables of the taverna. We decide on one overlooking the gorge so that we can look down to the rushing waterfalls and over the river to the chapel. The proprietor brings us water and a menu.

"You choose," I say.

"I'm not really used to this in a man", she says, "but I understand." She knows I cannot read, let alone understand, Greek.

We sit here, the only customers, arms resting on the table. "Happy?" she says.

The owner comes back with a bowl of green salad, full of cucumber and tomatoes and with a rectangular chunk of cheese on the top.

"Greek Salad," says Fotini, "Welcome to my country."

"I like the way we get served with water, almost before we have sat down. Is that normal here?"

"Doesn't it happen like that in England?"

We look at each other and laugh. There is so much that we don't know in practical terms, even if emotionally we are on the same plane.

We order another couple of beers and the proprietor, Γωργος, comes over to drink a beer with us. He and Fotini get into a long and serious conversation. Occasionally she breaks off from talking so that she can translate the gist of it to me. They are discussing in considerable detail the possibility of some form of armed conflict involving Greece. It is difficult to understand where they expect this threat to come from, but I know just about enough of the history of modern Greece to suspect that it is Turkey that they fear the most, although both Albania and Macedonia are in the running.

They seem almost resigned to there being a war. This is the first I have heard about it, certainly I have seen nothing about it in the British press. I wonder how they can be so calm, but then Greece was an occupied country for so much of its long and troubled history that it is no wonder that these modern Greeks seem to accept conflict as almost inevitable.

The meal is satisfying and we linger over it. Eventually Fotini goes off to have a pee and I do my best to understand Γωργος efforts to tell me how much I owe him. I have a feeling that he has been rather kind to us. I give the man a decent tip, but not too generous. I do not want to be thought of as a rich tourist, but I suppose that to Γωργος that is just what I am.

As wey are about to get into the car Fotini speaks to an old lady dressed entirely in the traditional black garb of a Greek widow. "She needs a lift to the village, is that okay with you?"

I nod and clear the back seat. The lady gets in the car and I drive up the gorge out onto the open moorland. We come to a fork and I swing right, knowing that to be the direction we came from. There is a murmuring from the back. Fotini turns to me and tells me wey have gone the wrong way, so I reverse the car and takes the left fork.

We stop at the outskirts of the village and their elderly passenger slides out of the car. It would have been nearly an hour's walk for her if we had not helped her on her way.

"That was really kind to suggest that," I say, turning to Fotini.

"Kindness is repaid with kindness. If we hadn't given her that lift we would have taken the wrong road. There is a purpose in things you know, sometimes we don't see it at the time, sometimes it's just so obvious."

And thus it was then, when our purpose, ourr way in life, did indeed seem obvious. But wrong roads are taken and, like those candles that were so lovingly placed together, their brightest dreams have long since guttered into their own darkness.

13

This Land, This People

Forum of antiquity
unflinchingly bearing
your ruination
in the heat and dust of
rapine excavation.
Wanton to a million shuffling sandals,
kicking, slipping, tripping,
over your exposed recumbence.
They take you, quite unheeding,
snapping at your attributes,
never pausing or inquiring.
For beyond the palatable,
sprawl the spawn of an older
Civilization, cast heedlessly
upon the wayside
Olympians to their last, and
gnarled as olive trees these
black-robed precursors of

the future stand,
slightly bending.
Worthy ancestors to
populations present,
protected by custom,
preserved by veneration,
parenting by pain those
long-dropped generations.
Fertility lies fecund in
the unturned folds of
red-earthed fields,
stretching themselves indolently,
from sea to mountain,
their harvest
willingly wishing to be
coaxed and stroked
into the yielding.
Nurtured of our ploughing,
our sowing, our tending
the beauty of this bounty lies
ready to be reaped.
Flesh-ripe sustenance, compliant
in the plucking,
becomes our swollen future
of hope and inspiration.
This produce of the present,
the juice of unforbidden fruit,
lies sweetly on
the lips.

14

Imagination

Hara is exhausting, and not a little crazy. I have come to live with her. I love her dearly, but not with the wildest of passions. I am undeniably fond of this tallish platinum blonde woman. She is intriguing with her extraordinary vivid imagination, and she is really very beautiful in a rather non-Greek way, tall and thin like a willow with her long almost white hair falling down to the small of her back.

Before we met we had Skype-ed. On one of these occasions Hara explained that she had suffered from a bout of ill health some four years ago and had taken up Turkish dancing as a way to restore both her body and her spirits.

"So, can you still remember how to do it?"

"Oh yes," she says, "would you like to see?" And without waiting for an answer she pulls up her white sweater to just below her tits and slips her jeggings to somewhere well south of her belly button "Enjoy," She says

She starts to gyrate moving her midriff in circles in a highly artistic and somewhat arousing manner. She goes faster whilst she gyrates, smiling all the time and making beckoning gestures towards her screen – and me. Proceedings are brought to a halt by her jeggings falling to her ankles.

"Whoops!" she says, displaying some very scanty white knickers and, rather to my dismay, lets her sweater drop whilst she recovers the rest of her clothing.

"Did you like that?"

She knows that I did. It only now, after I meet her that I discover that Hara's 'bout of ill health' was a pretty devastating nervous breakdown.

Hara is a one-off bundle of nerves, uninhibited and imaginative.

She lives in a fourth-floor apartment in an eastern suburb of Thessaloniki.. She explained to me how she had designed the layout herself when the place was being built working with builders to achieve just the space that she wanted. She had then furnished it to her own taste – and indeed it was pleasingly laid out including a large living room with a kitchen/diner alcove. This description of her prowess on the house renovating front was nothing other than 'Hara the Romancer'. She simply could not control herself. It wasn't that she told lies, just that the humdrum of existence was so tedious for her that she had to use her fertile imagination to enhance it a little. I later discovered that the apartment belonged to her son, Sotiris, and that he had bought it, fully furnished, from a friend long before Hara had seen it.

Hara needed her flights of fancy. It was, and is, her protection. A shield against an outer world of chaos and confusion. At the age of 17 she was married off to a rich Greek American whom she had only met twice. Her parents welcomed the 'good marriage' that they had so successfully arranged. She had been transported out to Florida within a week of the nuptials. There she was quite alone, with no friends and certainly no one who spoke her native Greek. She taught herself English by watching the commercials on American television. Perhaps such an introduction to the language further warped her attitude towards life.

The rich guy, her husband, impregnated her within the first few days of their marriage and then tired of her as soon as her belly started to expand. She, and her new-born son, Sotiris, were relegated to new quarters at the top of the house. Hara and her husband never had sex again, indeed they hardly spoke to each other. Eventually she managed to persuade him to let her and Sotiris, accompany him back to Greece on one of his visits to manage his various properties in Sithonia. When they arrived, she promptly 'escaped' with Sotiris to live with her mother in a small apartment in the unfashionable district of Iliopoli . She sued for divorce and took a job as a wholesale salesperson for cheap beach-type clothing which she enjoyed immensely. This kept her and Sotiris in funds whilst he grew up. The financial crisis came, the firm collapsed, Hara lost her job, and her son went to live with his father in the States.

Before we met in person, Hara had e-mailed me a grainy photo of herself on a beach. I had described her as looking like a 'Ghost in a Sandstorm'. She likes that description and often mentions it. She is very passionate. In her beach house, when we first have sex, she carefully shuts the bedroom door and turns to me. "What goes on in here when the bedroom door is shut is strictly between you and me," she said, "nothing we say or do with or to each other is for the outside world." I respect her wishes not least because she gave good reason for her demand for secrecy. I have never abused that trust.

We decide to set up home together, whilst we would keep the house in Thessaloniki we would also buy somewhere, most probably in Halkidiki. Just to be sure we also visit many seaside villages further down the opposite coast, under Olympus. But it is to Halkidiki that wey return.

"Let's go and have a look at Nikiti," she says one morning. "There are lots of lovely stone cottages above the main coast road, in the old town, and I know that you will just love them."

Wey do indeed look at some many houses. Hara discovers which properties might be for sale by chatting up taverna owners, jumping out of the car and asking people in the street, and knocking on doors of cottages that she likes the look of. It surprises me that more often than not the inhabitants are happy to discuss the possibility of selling their house, or at least knew of a neighbour that they think might be interested in doing so. She has a charm and confidence in her manner that many people find irresistible. Once or twice I get the impression that there is a lack of serious long-term commitment on her part, but she enters into the process of looking for a property with gusto. House Agent is one of her many 'roles'.

Whilst wearing her 'house hunting' hat Effie befriends a guy called Carlos who is manager of the local supermarket.

He in turn knows someone who works for the marketing co-operative for Sithonian honey.

Hara sees an opening.

She immediately takes it upon herself to adopt the role of Marketing Manager (Greece) for a thriving UK import/export company. She has been tasked with exploring opportunities with the Marketing Director (UK) who of course speaks no Greek. This multi-national firm is interested in food imports to the UK, and of course honey could be important in that context.

Carlos arranges for Hara and I to meet his 'honey contact' at a beach bar that evening and, following some phone calls, it is agreed that they would meet the MD of the honey co-operative the next day.

As all these arrangements have been made in Greek, I have very little knowledge of what is being discussed. I have no idea of the role that Hara has cast me in and that I am, at least in her reality, the MD of a large company. Perhaps I am being a little naïve, but I assume that Hara has organised a visit to the local honey co-operative so that I can see a different facet of Greek life.

This 'friendly visit' turns out to be a high-powered meeting in the Co-operative Board Room. Hara is at her best and is marvellous. She devours the statistics that they shower upon her and clearly impresses the Directors with 'our' marketing credentials. Every so often she speaks a few words to me that those present would have taken to be an accurate translation of proceedings. This they are not. Instead she tells me that she is explaining to them why I want to live in Greece. All the while she continues to negotiate production quotas and shipping costs with the Board.

The saving grace in this crazy and pointless deception is that the MD speaks very little English and thus my status as an important Import/Export agent is happily accepted. Hara plays up to her role wonderfully, mis-translating as I later discovered, my facile questions about the community life of the Queen Bee into searching enquiries about cost/benefit analysis and patents on logos. This could no doubt have gone on indefinitely, or at least until the 'boss' failed to produce a chequebook for a few hundred barrels of honey. However, the MD's secretary intervenes, she has been hovering in the background and casting suspicious glances in my direction. Now she has a brief whispered conversation with the MD. She must be the only person in the room, besides ourselves, who has any real grasp of the English language.

The MD rises to his feet saying, as translated to me later by a highly amused Hara, that in his opinion there is only a very limited market for Sithonian honey in the UK and that the meeting is therefore over, There is nothing for it but for the two of us to abandon our half-finished coffees and retire with as much dignity as is possible.

15

Piraeus Lunch

Rarely is a visiting Englishman as privileged as I. Of the millions of foreign visitors to the Greek capital how many experience the 'Real Greece'? Well, thanks to a delightful and extraordinarily hospitable Greek woman I have had just that experience.

You may wonder if I am talking of a tour of the Parthenon or a night out in the Plaka. No, far from it, I was given a much better time than either of these tourist honeypots could have provided me with, for I have had lunch in an ordinary apartment in a quiet corner if Piraeus. Nothing special, you understand, although it was so very precious for me. Good wholesome food and the company of a petite 50-something and her delightful mother.

I had met Vaso only a day or two before and with typical Greek openness she had, on learning that I wanted to experience the lives of ordinary, decent Greek people, invited me to her home. Had this happened in the U.K I would have assumed there was some hidden agenda, perhaps I would be assaulted and robbed by Vaso's accomplices, but here, in this impoverished and misrepresented country, honesty and decency prevail.

I sat in the rather cramped kitchen and watched as these two women, mother and daughter, in perfect harmony, created our meal, each seeming to know just what was wanted of them by the other. They were not embarrassed or concerned that I was sitting with them as they busied themselves with basic ingredients. It just seemed the most natural thing in the world that we three should be there together.

We ate satisfying, tasty and beautifully prepared food that was lovingly presented and accompanied by a bottle of rosé wine. It was not lost on me that this small feast, so kindly given, must have cost them rather more than a week of their normal lunches. But they looked shocked and distressed that I should have offered to pay for some of the ingredients. "But you are our guest," said Vaso, "an honoured visitor to my country, and you will pay nothing, nothing at all." She meant it. Such is the spirit of the people here.

When we had finished eating, I offered to help with the washing up, as I would in any such situation in England. They thought I was joking - apparently Greek males, especially visiting ones, do not sully themselves by dirtying their hands in the kitchen! So whilst Vaso cleared the table her mother, who did not speak a word of English, entertained me in the living room. This remarkable woman had been a child at the time of the German occupation of Greece. Her father had died when she was a toddler and her mother had left her in the charge of her late husband's daughter by an earlier marriage.

As a child and young girl Vaso's mother had thereafter been treated by her 'family' as an unpaid servant. This was a harsh upbringing even for those grim times. As a result, she had never learned to read or write. At a tender age she had been 'rescued' by marriage to a man many years her senior, but more hardship was to come for her husband had died only a few years after the marriage leaving her to bring up four young children entirely on her own. And from this awful combination of desperate of circumstances there was now, in front of my eyes, the most delightful, charming, and personable old lady that it has ever been my good fortune to meet.

When Vaso rejoined us her mother insisted that she should bring me a precious glass of Tsipouro made from grapes that had been lovingly gathered by the family from their own vineyard way up in the mountains of north-west Greece. It was so wonderful, not just the drink itself but the symbolism of this gift to a stranger, a foreigner, an Englishman in their midst. But the real treat was yet to come, for with little promoting from her daughter and no false modesty this wonderful old lady broke into a series of traditional country songs, songs of love and loss and longing, unaccompanied by any instrument. The cadences of her high-pitched melodic voice will remain with me forever.

Lunch over, Vaso and I strolled along the harbour front at Piraeus lined as it was with yachts as expensive as any you would find in Monaco. I looked at their Greek flags. "Not so much poverty here then?"

"The owners are our Greek elite," said Vaso with a bittersweet smile. "They helped our politicians into power so now our government helps them."

So, this is Greece, the Real Greece. To this place tourists do not penetrate, either physically or emotionally. It is also a place where taxes are paid only by those who can least afford to do so.

16

Plus ça Change

It had to stop. The noise that is, it was too much at this time of the morning. Yesterday the Municipality of Thessaloniki took it into its head to close off Proxenou Koromila and carry out a major suction exercise on the main sewers therein. Okay, so I have no doubt that it needed doing, but at 7 o'clock in the morning it was disturbing to a retired old man.

Today I lay in bed idly wondering if this new intrusion was an extension of yesterday. Certainly the sound was different, more like a man wielding a pickaxe, again and again and again. Perhaps one of the sewers was blocked and needed digging up? So, on it went, THUMP, THUMP, THUMP. Whoever was doing it must be getting pretty warm. Even at this time of the morning the temperature would have been approaching 20 degrees (that is just short of 70 degrees Fahrenheit to those of you, like me, who find Centigrade a bit of a thermal challenge!).

I am not, by nature, an early riser, but there was all too little hope of dozing off again until I had found out what was going on. I slipped from my bed and padded across the sitting room to the front balcony. There was a momentary hiatus as I pulled up the blind – to my potential embarrassment I realized I was stark naked. This unfortunate lapse remedied I paced across the balcony to the rail and peered down eight floors of apartment block at the miniscule street below. Nothing. There was just a car making its way to the 'Parking' and a couple of blokes walking in the other direction. No sign of anyone in a fit of macho fervor swinging iron at concrete.

And yet the noise continued, unabated. I looked to my left and there, a couple of floors beneath me on the far side of the road was a middle-aged woman knocking seven bells out of a carpet. Said carpet was trussed up over her balcony and she was laying into it with a large and fearsome carpet beater. She did not, even for one tiny moment, relent. With metronomic precision her arm flailed at the innocent carpet. She was too far away to be certain but I felt sure I could see bulging muscles under her light dress. My thoughts turned to her husband.

So, I mused, as I regained the sanctuary of my bed, it was mid-May and Spring-Cleaning time had come to Greece. All over this city, and no doubt elsewhere in the country, carpets were being hit, walls washed down, matrasses thumped, and everything in, or out of, sight being vacuumed.

Then there is the 'Carpet Holiday Syndrome'. You did not know that Greek carpets have a summer holiday? Nor did I until my friend texted me that she was 'having her carpet put into storage'. I asked if she had decided she did not like it. There followed one of those strange text conversations when neither side has a clue as to what the other is trying to say and assumes that they are just very stupid. Eventually we resolved this as being a culture-barrier thing. For the price of no more than €12 a firm will come in May and remove your sitting room carpet, clean it, and store it safely until you are ready for its return in October. In the meantime you are left with a lovely cool tiled floor for the summer.

With Carpet Holidays and Spring Cleaning comes a wardrobe change. Clothes of the summer months would be being reinstated in their wardrobes, whilst winter wear was banished to attic and cellar. The precise date of such frenzy may not be immutable but it has been borne upon me that the process by which a Greek, most particularly a Greek woman, changes her wardrobe is fast, sudden, and absolute. In March we had some lovely weather. I strolled along the Paralia in what to me seemed blazing sun. The temperature was in the high 20's (there I go again!) and the sky blue. Whilst forswearing shorts, as I did not wish to make too much of a spectacle of myself, I wore a short-sleeved shirt and thin trousers.

Not so my fellow strollers. Everyone was wearing coats. I do not mean the flimsy sort of thing that might adorn one on a mild summer evening, no we are talking Puffa jackets, great black padded affairs, designed to keep out snow and gales. At the onset of winter the street market vendors switch from selling cotton dresses to Puffa jackets. The change, in mid-October, is quicker than the blink of an eye and not dissimilar to the peripatetic vendors of umbrellas who are normally invisible but who appear in the streets as soon as the first drops of rain start to fall.

And then there are the boots. Stroll along Tsimiski in the winter and the multitude of shoe shops are stuffed full of black, tan, white, and brown boots of every length, design and price. Venture there at the end of May and a thousand boots have sounded the retreat and retired to their winter quarters, making way for shoes, and of course sandals.

I come from a part of England where it has been known to snow in June, and where 25 degrees is considered a heat-wave. The weather is driven mainly by a capricious Atlantic ocean that only occasionally gives way to a bubble of high pressure from the East; the weather changes; often. Thus we only have one wardrobe. We may have as many clothes as Greeks, but we need to reach for any of them at any time throughout the year. There is no closed season on Puffa jackets or boots. To this end it is helpful that most of us do not live in apartments, with their limited space for everyday clothes storage.

As that great British poet TS Elliot said (okay he was born in the States, but was an Anglophile and became a British citizen) 'April is the cruelest month'. And indeed here in Greece it is possible to see why. The weather will not yet have settled into its summer haze of sunshine and warmth. A lovely hot spell will be followed by a week of cold rainy days, indeed it is not unlike High Summer in England! And it is indeed cruel upon those that have two wardrobes. Fearful of the danger of too early a change most Greeks hang on until the middle of the following month before committing themselves to summer.

Thus it was that throughout the latter part of March and early April, when the weather was warm and dry here in Thessaloniki, that my fellow walkers were clad in full winter kit, more befitting to a snowy mountain hike than a sunny stroll along the Paralia. Poor things they had nothing else to wear.

There may however be another reason for such laggardly acceptance of summer. As I write the weather is gorgeous, the temperature in the shade is 28 degrees (okay 83 F) and there is a gentle breeze tugging playfully at my papers. However June is just around the corner and as that pleasing month draws to a hot end we have to face the daunting prospect of July and August. Urban Greece of course closes down for those two excruciatingly hot months. Everyone makes for the seaside and sanity to avoid 40 degrees and more (dear dinosaur, you are on your own now – that is well over 100 F, something totally alien to the British Isles). So there needs to be preparation for such heat, and one answer lies in acclimatization.

If you feel a bit hot in April whilst clad in your Puffa jacket. If your feet are a bit sweaty, tucked snugly into long warm boots, then this is but the merest foretaste of August in Greece. Best that you get used to it or your very survival will be at stake. Nevertheless I claim exemption by Englishness. I will wear my shorts and sandals just as the weather dictates, and when July bears down upon me in its full rage, then I will find an accommodating beach house and go and sit in the gloriously warm Aegean sea and be oh so happy that I am part of this wonderful country.

17

The Man

The place smelt of rotting fish. A paradise for Greek street cats but hardly the right ambiance for this occasion. Mind you the venue was hardly inspiring either, being the nether end of a municipal car park in a one of the rather less salubrious suburbs of Thessaloniki.

"Do you want to come to a meeting at Stavroupoli this evening?"

I had told Eleni that I was doing nothing else and would be delighted to do so.

"Okay, catch a 27 from Egnatia and I will meet you by the Town Hall at a quarter to eight."

With foresight I had anticipated the rain, equipping myself with a small black brolly. What I had not anticipated was the cold. I had been sitting in an abandoned bus shelter for some three quarters of an hour awaiting the arrival of my companion and guide. The chill that was eating into my marrow was testament to the vagaries of a mid May evening in Greece.

A street beggar sidled up and sat at the far end of my bus shelter bench. He was dark-skinned and evinced a crippled walk that might have been genuine. His brown suit was ripped and stained, although no doubt in the distant past it had been the pride of its tailor. He wore a red bobble hat. We hardly glanced at each other but perhaps there was a slight kinship, an abandoned Englishman and an abandoned destitute. We did not speak.

People were arriving. Some in smart business suits, others in casual evening wear. Many seemed to know each other, there was a lot of handshaking, hugging and cheek-kissing. Most of the women wore tights and skimpy dresses. I shivered. They did not.

The car park was shunned, apparently the pavement was the place for parking, and that in as chaotic a manner as possible. Then Eleni was squeezing her rather dirty black Nissan between a motor cycle and a lamp post. She greeted me with a thousand apologies, however it was obvious to me that I had been early, having arrived only fifteen minutes after the allocated start time. We ventured towards the noisy, and by now fairly crowded end of the parking lot. It was getting dark. The rain was just slightly heavier.

A huge picture at the back of the makeshift staging was a masterpiece of PR, depicting a firm but benign grey-bearded, smiling man holding a kid. Umpteen decibels of Greek music were pouring forth from a great tower of speakers draped rather fetchingly against the rain in a green polythene wrap. From this strange looking alien backdrop emerged a quivering amplification of sound that drowned any attempts at serious communication. As each track ended the MC would announce in Greek "In just a few minutes we will be joined . . . by . . . YOUR VERY OWN CURRENT AND FUTURE MAYOR." At which there were would be a great roar of acclaim and the sounding of car horns. The absence of The Man following each of these announcements served to encourage rather than disappoint the damp but cheerful crowd.

Rows of white plastic seats had appeared from nowhere. We made our way towards them with purpose. I certainly had no intention of standing for the next hour. Eleni knew, and greeted, so many people that our progress towards said seats was slow, and finally arrested by the appearance of Arsenoi, complete with her sister. There were more hugs and handshakes and kisses. Shouting over the music Eleni explained that the Mayor had, at her suggestion, appointed Arsenoi as his deputy. Arsenoi was clearly pleased about this. She was handing out encapsulated pictures of herself to pin on the lapels of her supporters. I managed to avoid such labelling.

We sat. Above the roar of the music I shouted to Eleni. "So this is Greek politics?"

"It used to be much bigger than this," she said. "The new system of Mayoral elections just might revive the old tradition that has been spoiled by television, YouTube and suchlike. These political rallies are not what they were."

"When is the election?"

"The day after tomorrow, Sunday," she said.

But now The Man was amongst us. Strangely the 'real life' Mayor looked just like the enormous publicity picture that loomed over him. He worked the front row with handshakes then responded to the MC's introduction by mounting the stage and standing at the lectern beaming at us.

For forty minutes this man spoke. He spoke without notes, and he spoke well. My Greek is such that I understood but little of what he said, however that hardly mattered for the stuff of his talk was that of all politicians. He used his voice well, he was clear, he spoke seriously and then light-heartedly, and he roused his audience as he tackled his major issues. They loved it. From time to time, and prompted by the cognoscenti in the front row, they clapped and hooted and shouted their approval. The Man deserved to win on Sunday based on volume alone. Finally, exhibiting all of the 'hwyl' of a Welsh preacher, his voice rose to breaking point as he made his final plea to 'Vote early and vote often'. Well, I think that is what he said, perhaps my Greek failed me?

For the past half hour my thoughts had been turning towards the nearby bar, so it was borne upon me with some displeasure that despite The Man having stood back from the lectern the show was not yet over. One half of what I had assumed was an audience composed of the general public now left its seats and swarmed forward, a great horde of people surging across the front of the area towards the steps of the stage. Meanwhile The Man had received a bunch of flowers from a pretty little girl – as witnessed by the intensity of the flash photography. Now one by one, with the MC calling their names, this great crowd of people filed up on stage to be hand-shaken, hugged and kissed by The Man.

"Who are they?" I mouthed to Eleni.

"His Deputies," she replied.

Oh, so Arsenoi was just one Deputy amongst this hoard. Well not quite, because once the stage had filled up to breaking point the first tranche of fifty deputies was dismissed, and the Great Man set about welcoming the second tranche to the now empty stage. Arsenoi's moment was just that: move forward, handshake, hug, double cheek-kiss, then make way for the next. A last, it was over. The music blared out, and the stagehands swiftly parted us from our chairs. The Man was pumping the flesh. I was introduced as a colleague from England. In my best Greek I said I was sorry I was not registered to vote. His mouth smiled at me. His eyes did not. We went our separate ways.

I needed a drink. I also needed information. We sat in the bar that I had been eyeing all evening. To my persistent questioning Eleni explained that there were one hundred deputies who, if The Man were to be elected, would compete for council seats, of which there were 40. Apparently The Man was not of any political party but an independent, as are many such mayoral candidates. Such Independents elicit support from one or more of the established parties, but are not of those parties. Eleni seemed surprised when I asked about his policies.

"Oh, we don't bother about that sort of thing," she said, "We just vote for him because he is our friend, we like him, and he will look after us."

I wondered about this. Much as I deplore the state of party politics in the UK, I have a sinking feeling that if the heads of local government in Greece are elected on the basis of being supported by their friends and families, then there is the expectation of a favour to be repaid. Furthermore, wherever The Man's rhetoric had led him and his supporters this evening no one in his audience seriously considered his words to be electoral promises. It was the show that mattered, the bonding experience, the bonding of expectations.

I applaud the idea of electing independent candidates, thereby slipping the straightjacket of party politics. But in voting for such I would prefer to back a well-balanced and immutable policy agenda that the candidate feels obliged to implement.

Now The Man was working our bar. He slapped men on the back, he nodded sagely as individuals bent his ear, he even kissed the scantily dressed waitress who was in much more danger of revealing the deliciously rounded parts of her body than The Man was of revealing his politics. He even sat, albeit briefly, and probably by mistake, at our table. And then he was gone.

Perhaps I am wrong. It is arguable that local government should be conducted on the basis of who knows who and what favours are owed. At the very least it is friendlier than the UK system, and in a strange way more open. What is more, it seems to work – as well as anything ever does in Greece!

18

Still Waiting

With a nod to C P Cavafy.

Do I yet await the Barbarians,
sitting by your the gates in such fine array?
Half-held hopes are but fleeting talismans
against this judgement of the final day.
Are the trumpets now sounding the alarm?
(cast a glance to see if they are come!)
No defences can shield ourselves from harm.
(Can you see their dust? Do you hear their drum?)

If only Conscience had beaten and flayed
this Vanity that all but smothers guilt,
past-inflicted wounds the mind barricades
would be disowned dreams, buried to the hilt.

No Barbarians came; they never will?
It's a waiting game. I am waiting still.

19

Greek Bathrooms

Greek bathrooms are an afterthought. Indeed 'Bathroom' is hardly the correct term for these dark dingy little holes that lurk betwixt the washing machine and the security door in Greek apartments. Very few of these stale-aired pits boast an actual bathtub. Those that once might have aspired to such decadence now sport a tub that has long since shed any pretence of being enamelled. I suppose they do install baths with plugs, but these handy objects must spirit themselves away into the night, never to be replaced.

In tourist hotels the visitor is lulled into complacency by the glistening marble of the walls and the 'sanitized' loo seat of the en-suite. A small notice, possibly in English, stating that you must not put paper down the bog is the only indication that Greek plumbing is of a startlingly primitive nature. This is all too obvious outside such a sheltered environment

I had misguidedly rented a flat in Kato Toumpa. As far as apartments in Thessaloniki suburbs go it wasn't that bad. It is true that the walls needed a very substantial coat of paint and the furniture would have purpose if the Greeks celebrated 5th November with a roaring bonfire. There was a curious lack of any electric sockets in the kitchen, and the absence of air conditioning did not bode well for the heat of the summer. Nevertheless it would have been survivable, had it not been that 'bathroom'.

Yes, there was a bathtub. I eyed it with distaste. The whole of its lower surface was a uniform grey colour. It was not only filthy but, should I be brave enough to sit in it, my nether regions faced the prospect of being rubbed down with something akin to grade 40 sandpaper.

There was a catholic collection of pipes and tubes, some copper, some plastic, and a couple of flexible steel things. They looped and sagged around the room in a contortion of amorous webs. Some ended abruptly, others disappeared into holes broken into the plasterwork.

I have encountered many weird and some decidedly insanitary lavatory pans in my travels, but this innocent looking white receptacle, aligned at an indecisive angle between washing machine and basin, contained within in its murky depths that which I think it best to draw a veil over. Suffice it to say that a month of scrubbing with the most vicious concoction of chemicals available from the local supermarket made no impression at all upon this Thing.

The basin was new. It gleamed at me, smugly from its lair, an ancient cabinet. Incongruously green I discovered that it possessed an evil nature by virtue of the absence of any form of overflow. Thus whilst concentrating upon the morning shave it was all too easy to leave the water running just enough to quickly fill this shallow beast. It then began to surreptitiously discharge itself with fearsome accuracy in the direction of what might politely be termed my lower belly. A creeping dampness was the first indication of a soaking patch of embarrassment that called for a change of trousers and underwear.

Clearly I needed to move house. Indeed had the bathroom been spotless I would have felt compelled to move Basecamp Gordon from such an unedifying location. Those born and bred in this nondescript suburb will no doubt seek to die with the words 'Kato Toumpa' carved indelibly upon their hearts. But less committed mortals would find it hard to find many kind words for this product of the lack of post-war building policies. So the search was on for pastures fresh. I eschewed all locations save those in the very centre of Thessaloniki. If I was indeed going to live in this city then I was not going to suffer another Kato Toumpa.

The system for letting apartments in this country is fine, if you are born and bred in Thessaloniki. I wasted a couple of weeks scouring the internet, finding pleasant properties, and phoning Agents whose English was almost as doubtful as my Greek. It took me that fortnight to realize that these advertised properties had long since been let and are left on the 'net as some form of promotion. It is possible to discover Real Estate offices, but few have what I would regard as a normal shop front. Most are located on the first or second floor of apartment blocks. Gaining access to such is a minor challenge, especially if the main door is locked and you are presented with an array of names, all in Greek, without reference to the company name of the Agent. The only solution I could find was to ring each bell in turn and asked the disembodied voice that barked from the intercom if it spoke English. This would result in a tirade of Greek – that might, or might not, be entirely friendly. Occasionally the door release button would be pressed. Access thus achieved it was simply a matter of wandering up the stairs, stopping at each floor to peruse nameplates.

Once in the hands of an Agent it is difficult to wriggle free. This is due partly to the crisis, but mainly because the client pays half the Agent's fee. The Royal Institution of Chartered Surveyors would no doubt frown upon such practice, for the Agent becomes a two-faced go-between, acting for both seller and buyer. The Agent therefore likes to get to know you, the process is however a very friendly one. My visits to properties were interspersed with multiple sojourns in cafes that involved lengthy discussions about things sporting, cultural and amorous. Indeed I played chess in a bar for three hours with one Agent. He beat me, twice. Work in Greece is a way of life and is best treated as a pleasure.

Although I had not found a new place I was desperate to leave Kato Toumpa. I needed to escape the two-year contract that I had, foolishly, signed. I invented a sick relative in the UK and went to see my landlord's solicitor. We had a friendly discussion in partly Greek, partly in English but mostly in French in his office, just off Aristotelous. We drank coffee, we discussed Europe, we drank more coffee, we talked about things literary, I signed something foregoing my deposit, and after a final coffee I walked out the door a Free Man. I had just two weeks to find an apartment or I would be joining the down and outs in sleeping on a park bench.

The days ticked away all too fast. My friends helped me to look at possible places, but none were suitable, I sensed a mild feeling of rising panic. Then I struck gold, a penthouse just behind the Paralia. So that Saturday evening I was sitting in the plush downtown office of my putative landlord who was happily bending the Greek taxation laws to breaking point. I would sign an agreement to rent her property that would involve 'paying' a very small rent to a family company in Cyprus. In reality I would pay a rather more substantial amount from my UK bank to a cash-collection in her name at Western Union. She would furnish the apartment for me with the essentials – except for a bed – and I would take the electricity in my name. We drank coffee. We shook hands. The Deal was done. There were just three days to get the new apartment into shape and get myself moved.

My excellent landlord was as good as her word and a modicum of furniture arrived on the Monday morning. I needed a bed. I girded my loins and set off by bus to IKEA, emerging three hours later the owner-to-be of a bed and other flat-pack sundries. The convolutions, in Greek, of getting the items picked for me, delivered, and then hoisted to the eighth floor were extreme, but success was achieved and by the next day I had negotiated the Allen-key assembly and thus had a double bed to collapse upon. But I had no electricity.

It was moving day. My chess-playing agent offered to transport my suitcases, computers and cleaning things from Kato Toumpa. He arrived in the smallest filthiest car that ever graced a Greek road and we squeezed everything, and ourselves into it. Door to door delivery was achieved by halting the car in the single-file one-way street and divesting it of cases, bags, and packages. In the meantime those whose automotive passage was being thus hindered sounded a cacophony of frustration.

Being without power meant no light, no heat, and no cooking. I was in desperate need of electricity and a visit to the local DEH office was clearly indicated. Clutching my signed and stamped copy of the false lease I braved this peculiarly Greek institution. Flashing red lights indicated the progress of what looked like three different queues. I fumbled a Greek question and was dismayed to learn that I needed the 'B' queue. A machine spat out my number – 103 – they were currently dealing with number 63. A coffee was called for

Half an hour later I returned to find that they had reached 97. I sat down to wait, and to cogitate upon this arcane system of becoming an electricity customer. No chance of a quick phone call, or an online application. Here it was footwork and waiting - a return to the age of steam. I duly waited.

When your turn comes it is no good being caught napping. You have to be quick. If you do not go to the booth indicated by the flashing reds within about 10 seconds the next customer is called and you lose your place. I made it, but only just. The clerk did not speak English. Our business was conducted mainly by mime. Production of passport, AFM and stamped lease was sufficient to ensure the creation of two pages of small print – in Greek – that the clerk and I both signed. Only one more queue – to hand over a deposit of

€130 and electricity was to be mine by that evening. And the extraordinary thing was that I was indeed relieved from cold and starvation before nightfall.

I have strayed from bathrooms. I have been distracted by the intricacies involved in the abandonment of the Black Hole of Kato Toumpa and thus ensuring my continuing presence in this land fit for an Odyssey. I revelled in the glory of the shiny successor to the Black Hole. It walls glinted with marble. The floor gleamed with mosaic There was a faux-Gold tap arrangement for the bath. And yet . . . this was a Greek bathroom, and the tub, for it had a splendid tub, had two large and totally inexplicable chips in its enamel.

Whilst exhibiting none of the malevolence of the late, and unlamented, Black Hole, this Shiny Palace possessed a warped sense of humour that ensured its place amongst Greek bathrooms. I stripped to the buff, eager to shower my pink and substantial body. I clutched my sponge and wrapped myself, somewhat imperfectly, in in a towel and flung open the glass shower door to step in.

I reeled back.

This was no shower, but a Gordon Trap. It was an internal flue. Had I continued my progress it would have deposited me eight floors lower down in a crumpled heap.

Despite this I love Shiny Palace. But it is still an afterthought, a small and unloved intrusion into the architectural scheme of things. In the UK I luxuriate in a well-carpeted bathroom, scattered with candles and having a pleasing view from two large windows. I will forever be frustrated by the inability of Greek architects to adopt the concept of designing bathrooms that are fit for purpose.

20

Greek Dentists

My tooth hurt. An errant filling had succumbed to something sweet and sticky at the end of a meal in a delightful taverna in the Laladika district. Long ago the tooth had been drilled and filled in an English surgery with the rather half-hearted financial assistance that the National Health Service disburses. Dentists were more quick-witted than doctors when faced with a nascent NHS, and managed to retain much of their independence and thus most of their income.

Anyway this was Greece. No NHS here. I needed to 'go private'. There is a wayward charm about many Greek institutions. During my time in Thessaloniki I have encountered Citizens' Offices (KEPs), Police Stations, Health Centres, Electricity Offices, Taxation Offices, Aliens Bureaux and a myriad of other wonderful bastions of bureaucracy no doubt dating back to a certain Bavarian sense of order, but in spirit at least perhaps more akin to Byzantian times. I had however failed to experience the intricacies of dental practices in this wonderful country. It was time to change this.

Fortunately I was in possession of a card from a dentist, having met her some months previously when looking for an apartment to rent. I phoned Sofi and spoke to her directly, no receptionist. Yes, of course she remembered me, and yes indeed she would be delighted to sort my filling out, would tomorrow be soon enough?

Finding her surgery was not that easy. In England surgeries either occupy a whole building or, at the very least, the ground floor. This is not the case in Greece. At twelve-thirty I found myself at the entrance of a very ordinary apartment block, confronted by an array of doorbells. Next each of these was a nameplate. This should have posed no problem, except the names were all displayed in the Greek alphabet and with the Christian name being reduced to just an initial. They gave no clue as to whether that person was a lawyer, an estate agent, or a private individual. Certainly there was no indication of dentistry.

With the help of Sofi's business card I found her name, Σ. Παπαδιμητρου, and pushed the appropriate bell. I was admitted without conversation and took the stone staircase to the first floor. I found the appropriate door, which again opened immediately to my ring. I was in a waiting room. The walls were a pleasing but slightly shabby shade of green. Some pictures of old Thessaloniki added to the slightly down-at-heel appearance of the room. There was no discernible evidence that a receptionist had ever held domain over the place. Through from this waiting area there was the sound of happy chatter that did not seem to be interspersed with dental pauses.

I sat down on a chaise that proved to be so much more comfortable than its appearance suggested. The magazines provided were inclined towards the artistic and the historical, and despite being in Greek provided a welcome change from the facile publications that have bedevilled my past experiences of waiting rooms.

In fact this was not quite my first experience of Greek dentists. On an earlier occasion it had been my friend, Hara, who needed treatment. She had chipped a front tooth. It was too late to phone her downtown dentist that day despite the late working hours of such practices in Greece. She phoned early the next morning to make an appointment.

"One thirty tomorrow would suit me very well."

The following day we left the apartment just before 11.30. Along the harbour-front traffic was light and we made good time, even finding a parking space without undue difficulty. We had over an hour to kill, but this would be no problem as long as I could keep Hara from thinking about her broken tooth. She must have been looking for a suitable distraction herself.

"Let's go to the Hondos Centre," she said.

"Honda?" I said, wondering why on earth she wanted to look at Japanese cars. "Are you thinking of getting one?"

Hara looked at me oddly. "What on earth are you talking about Gordon?"

"This Honda Centre" I said, with only marginally dented confidence, "presumably they have the very best selection of used cars there?"

She burst out laughing. "You are a clown. It has nothing to do with Honda cars. Hondos Centres are beauty shops."

Skin-conditioner duly purchased there was still time for a Greek coffee, but moments later Hara jumped decisively to her feet, leaving her cup untouched "We must go."

Just a few paces and a lift ride later we entered the fourth-floor surgery. A bored looking receptionist had her head buried in a celebrity magazine as we entered. She looked puzzled at Hara's mention of her appointment.

"You can't have, not today."

"It was Hara's turn to look nonplussed. "But I phoned yesterday and was told to come at 1.30 today."

"Well that's impossible. He is not working in town this Friday."

"So how was I given a booking at 1.30," said Eri. "What's happened?"

With a great show of resentment the receptionist made a couple of phone calls. Apparently Hara had been booked into the dentist's surgery in Serres, a town about an hour's drive from Thessaloniki.

One of the many things I like about Greeks is their inability to suppress their emotions. A long and noisy 'conversation' ensued between Hara and the receptionist along the lines:

"It is entirely your fault. You never said you wanted the Thessaloniki surgery."

"Of course I didn't. He is always here on Fridays, I'm not an idiot!"

"Not this week. He changed his schedule, and it was very stupid not to say exactly what you wanted."

"Well how was I supposed to know that? You are a complete disaster!"

I intervened with as much aplomb as I would have mustered to achieve a ceasefire between two alley cats.

"Come on, Hara, it's time to go."

She wheeled upon me and I feared that I would be next to incur her wrath. Instead she grasped my hand and made for the door, all the time muttering things about 'malakas' in the general direction of the receptionist.

"Yas sas," intoned the far from subdued receptionist, and for my benefit "Have a Nice Day." Clearly she had learned her English in The States.

But here I was, sitting in the waiting room of a different surgery where the dentist was quite clearly present. Indeed the conversation in the next room was at this very moment rising to a note of farewell. A middle-aged and happy looking lady came through into the waiting room, wrapped a shawl around herself, and left. Sofi emerged from her sanctum, a sprightly and fit-looking 60-something, and kissed me on both cheeks. It was a decent way to be greeted by one's dental practitioner.

The surgery, if it could be thus described was wonderful. Yes there was a reclining chair, but it was upholstered in dark leather whilst the ubiquitous drill whose arms hovered above it was a thing from a 1960's film set. The walls were hung with pictures. Not, you understand, of cavities or dismal dental sets, but family photos of people enjoying themselves at the seaside. Alongside The Chair ran a long red mahogany cabinet that might, or might not contain dental implements. Atop it was a catholic mixture of old -ashioned sterilizer, glass jars, flowers, and framed photos.

The large bay window looked out onto the street. There was a slightly threadbare carpet that covered most of the floor, whilst a dark oak desk with a reed-backed chair complemented the comfortable feel of this far from modern surgery.

Sofi was clearly a competent professional, but it was equally obvious that she considered dentistry to be an essentially social affair. We chatted for some time about my stay in Greece, about The Crisis, about my writing, and about a mutual friend, so it was some time before I was bidden to The Chair. To my surprise Sofi sat on a chair between my reclination and the cabinet. I could see that she was within easy reach of the activators for the doorbell and the phone – a real one-man (or rather woman) show. I searched my memory of dental treatments past and concluded that I had never before been treated by a seated dentist.

Whilst my problem tooth hardly warranted it there did not seem to be the option of a pain-killing injection. I could see no evidence of a syringe, and being somewhat fearful of such devices I am pretty sure that I would have seen the signs of such had they existed. Sofi did the usual picking thing, chattering away all the while.

She reached for the drill. "Don't be afraid," she said. I cannot remember that being said to me by a dentist, even as a child.

Whilst she wielded her drill Sofi told me that she was no longer practicing.

I frowned and said, "Aghhh?"

"What I mean is that I am trying to retire, but from the time I stopped earning it takes nearly two years before I am paid any pension."

I tried to look as sympathetic as one can when assailed by mouth cramps "Aghhh," I said again.

"The deal is that you must stop work, then apply for your pension, then wait. So I am not working – officially – but how can I survive without any income?"

The black economy of Greece owes much of its existence to the ridiculous demands of an outdated bureaucracy. Happily for her I think that Sofi's pension must have through fairly shortly after that, for her phone was 'unavailable' a few months later when I tried to contact her.

This time I had lost no less than three fillings and my UK dentist had told me that each of these teeth were now finished, and that I would need implants for each at a cost of about £3,500 per tooth. I had told him that this was ridiculous and that I would take a second opinion – in Greece. He in turn had warned me that if I was treated in Greece I should not expect any help from him 'when it all goes wrong'. And so here I was back in Greece, needing treatment and without Sofi to provide it.

Salvation came in the form of Stavros. His surgery was towards the western side of town, just below Ano Poli. I walked past motorbike repair shops, and scruffy looking places with second-hand electrical goods spilling out onto the pavement. To my right a flashing neon sign spelled out the name 'Tobacco Hotel'. Even in this country of smokers it seemed a curious name, and one unlikely to elicit many bookings.

Entrance to Stavros' surgery was not dissimilar to Sofi's, although his waiting room boasted an enormous fish tank wherein two large and one small fish were circulating. I feared for the longevity of the small one.

Stavros took one look at the remnants of my teeth and declared that my NHS English dentist was totally misguided and that far from requiring implants matters could be sorted out by inserting a few pins and fillings at a cost of no more than €150 per tooth.

He was an interesting man, well-travelled and fluent in many languages. He had studied dentistry in France and Romania before returning to Greece and setting up his practice in this neighbourhood of Thessaloniki. He told me that he had instigated a quixotic scheme whereby the local people paid him just €10 euro a month for all the dental treatment they might need. He clearly enjoyed his dentistry, looking upon it almost as an art form, especially when 'sculpting' a replacement tooth. He could have made his fortune from practicing in a richer area of town with well-to-do clients. Instead he adopted a more philanthropic approach, and not only was clearly a benefactor to the locals, but a much more fulfilled man for so doing.

Like Sofi he treated me from a seated position and during the course of prolonged treatment only used a numbing injection on one occasion. He was dismissive of the extensive use of injections by UK dentists, suggesting that by such use they covered up their own dental clumsiness.

Also like Sofi, Stavros was also a 'one man band', having neither receptionist nor dental nurse, and needing neither. Actually that was not quite true. During his expert drilling, shaping and colouring of my new teeth I became aware that there was a third presence in the surgery. Gentle rustling sounds and indistinct mutterings were to be heard. I was curious, very curious.

My treatment having been successfully completed, and monetary transactions having been concluded – in 'black' cash of course – I ventured to enquire about the mysterious 'presence'. With a grin Stavros wheeled out a covered container. I assumed he was going to reveal some form of recording device. Instead he whipped of the blue cloth revealing a gloriously coloured and very large parrot.

"Wow," I said.

"Meet Yannis," said Stavros.

"Cawwww," said Yannis.

I am now the proud possessor of three excellently repaired teeth, and a beautiful parrot feather.

One year later 'Yannis' laid an egg – so her name is now Yanna

21

Greek Lifts

Vertical living is very much a part of life in almost any Greek city. The population rush from country to town during the latter part of the twentieth century put immense pressure on places such as Thessaloniki. The answer was to build high-rise apartment blocks, and it was thus with undisguised glee that the developers of the 1960's addressed the delightful exercise of filling their pockets with enormous amounts of money at minimal expense. Apartment-ville had arrived.

Initially the inclusion of a personnel lift in apartment development plans, if indeed such plans existed, seemed an unwarranted expense. But realisation dawned upon these fly-by-night entrepreneurs that it was not easy to sell an eighth floor apartment that could only be accessed by a staircase. And so the lift became a necessity. The architectural challenge was to fit this awkward vertical column into the building without losing too much valuable real estate. Lifts are therefore exceedingly small, inevitably confined to slightly obscure dark corners, and as a result rather smelly. Furthermore they have most certainly not been designed to complement their surroundings.

The rather more upmarket apartment block entrances in downtown Thessaloniki were designed to impress their parvenu clientele. They therefore boast marble walls, perhaps some mosaic decoration and a large gilded mirror or two. There might be an ornate commissionaire's desk, and a rack of dark oak carved pigeonholes awaiting communications of business and love. This was of course but an architectural ideal, and was soon overtaken by the practicalities of usage. There was no money for the commissionaire, the mosaic was done on the cheap, so started to 'moult' chips within a couple of years. The marble remains solidly intact, but the post pigeonholes stare out blankly and longingly, awaiting just one letter that would justify the expense of their installation. The post is left lying helplessly upon some latter-day installed cheap shelf where it is irregularly sifted by passing residents. The resulting heaps of unrecognised mail, glossy brochures advertising take away meals, and unrequited delivery slips, gaze blankly at the ceiling or slide, unwanted, to the floor.

But into this original concept of an elegant and imposing entrance there had to be fitted an uncompromisingly utilitarian element, the lift. Sometimes it was indeed an afterthought, in which case a degree of understanding can be extended to the necessary reorganisation of the stairwell. But since 1970 there really has been no such excuse as from then on the lift was firmly established as an integral part of the development, if not the design. But architects did not, understandably, welcome the harsh aesthetic offered by this device, so the wretched little orifice of the metal door had to be hidden somewhere, preferably at the back of the foyer, looped lovingly within the embrace of a stone staircase. Sometimes it is necessary to ascend to a mezzanine level in order to find the darn thing, for the interior designer would want nothing to detract from his vision of a grand staircase leading enticingly into the heart of his supposedly elegant building. But even then there was an overwhelming compunction to hide that bleak exterior with its prison-door window giving a frosted glimpse of the lighted cell within.

It therefore takes time, and not a little persistence, to locate the object of your ascending desire and to stab hard, probably several times at the unresponsive call button. There is a wayward streak amongst the system designers of lift electronics that no doubt has them gripping their sides with mirth after a hard day in the development lab. The pressing of the call button sets in motion a series of unplanned and unexpected events that involves the lift passing your entry point on at least one occasion before finally coming to rest with a chirpy 'ping'. At this stage you must act with determination and haste. Do not expect the lift door to open for you, instead you must grab it before the lift realises that it has made serious error in acceding to your wishes and decides to take itself off to the seventh floor where it can skulk unmolested by would-be users.

Most likely there will be a step to negotiate, either up or down depending upon the lifts proclivity of the day. It would seem that the elementary process whereby you set a lift to stop precisely at the level of the intended floor is either totally beyond the capabilities of Greek lift designers, or simply another little joke from the repertoire of those that laughingly call themselves lift service engineers. Do not be alarmed! It is unlikely that, once having stopped within a few hundred millimeters of the precise level, the lift will take it into its head that it should correct itself; unlikely, but not impossible.

The lift will be small, that is small in the sense of microscopic. No self-respecting dog would accept a kennel of such limited floor area. This then is no place to develop claustrophobia, indeed I cannot see how claustrophobics could exist above the second floor of a Greek apartment block. Should you be intending to travel upwards with a companion then the experience will be disgustingly or delightfully intimate, depending upon your joint relationship. Clearly the manufacturers of lifts realize that they are offering a spatially challenged environment and, in an attempt to alleviate the situation, have taken to installing mirrors that may grace one complete side of the lift. You therefore have the dubious pleasure of watching a reflection of yourself, and possibly your companion, as you rise or fall through the building.

It will no doubt come as a shock to those from abroad to discover that there is no inner door. The outer door will swing shut and you will find yourself staring in a rather puzzled way at its nether side. Do not worry. Brace yourself and hit the button for the floor you want. You may have to do this once or twice more before, with a despairing leap skywards, the lift decides it might as well take some vague notice of the electronic command. Now at this stage it is highly advisable on safety grounds to shrink back towards the rear of the lift. You may wish to do this in a nonchalant manner so as not to alarm your companion, especially if he or she is a Greek Lift Virgin. The reason for such action is that the lift will now be travelling at speed, well not much speed, more of a trundle, but the forward face of the lift, being bereft of anything even remotely door-like is now giving access to what in relative terms is a rapidly descending blank wall. There is nothing, except your sense of self-preservation, to stop you from reaching out and touching this inner face of the lift shaft. A further word of warning here. Some lifts are devilishly designed to debouche their occupants both front and rear. It is therefore quite possible that the 'back' of the lift will also be an open aperture with the shaft wall moving relative to you!

The experience is moderately interesting. If nothing else you will get a fairly good idea of the construction materials employed in the building of your apartment block. On slightly more upmarket shafts the walls are lined with metal. This gives poster stickers and graffiti artists a better substrate. I suppose they push the 'STOP' button between floors in order to ply their trade, I would however advise against this – not the creative graffiti bit you understand, but the stopping of the lift between floors. It may take a perverse liking to the location and decide to take up residence there.

At some stage in the fairly recent past it seemed that the Greek government had turned the corner and become safety conscious to the extent that they passed legislation obliging all lift owners to fit inner doors. There was hardly a flurry of activity. There is little heed taken here of legislative matters of this ilk, indeed I am not aware of any inner doors being fitted to existing lifts although they became rather more common on new ones. No one was indicted for failing to comply with the law, except the Minister responsible for the drafting of it who, so it transpired, had a controlling interest in the manufacturing company that sold inner doors to lift companies. I am not sure if the law has ever repealed. It is perhaps best described as 'inactive legislation'.

When you arrive at your intended floor, or perhaps I should say 'if the floor you have arrived at is your intended one', then all you have to do is to push hard against the outer door and you are debouched into a dark corridor. I mean dark in the sense that there is likely to be no light whatsoever. There will be, somewhere more or less opposite you, a light push switch. It is not easy to find although some nowadays glow with LED satisfaction. Be careful. It is very easy to mistake a doorbell for a light-push. This leads to Angry Words with owners of said doorbell who are thus disturbed from their cooking, snoozing, eating, or such other private activities as they may be indulging in.

However, thanks to Greek builders who watched too many 1970's American movies our lift has one more trick up its sleeve. There are certain whole-floor apartments where the lift opens directly into the flat rather than have you access it by means of a corridor. Under these circumstances the lift door does not open when you push it. This provides a certain frisson of excitement to the lift experience. If you are a visitor then the situation is quite simple. You should find a small bell-push set into the outer door and a shove on this will, with any luck, alert your host to open the imprisoning door for you from inside the flat. Should the bell not ring or should your host tarry a while before attending to you, then the lift is prone to tire of standing still and will no doubt decide to wander off to other floors taking you with it.

If you are the occupier of the apartment and are arriving at your door by means of the lift then you need to have your wits about you. No doubt you will have a key, either a simple latchkey or one of those over-sophisticated four-turn security affairs. Be sure to have it at the ready before your lift pauses at your apartment door. 'Pauses' is without doubt the correct word. You have a matter of seconds within which you must act. If you fail to engage the key then the lift is still 'live' and will happily respond to any summons from a different floor. Only by inserting your key can you be sure that the lift will not depart just as you finally push open your flat door.

Departure from such an apartment is fraught with further complication and as a prophylactic measure I would advise that you hold the key of the door in your hand as you enter the lift, for there is a very strong likelihood the lift will stubbornly refuse to budge once you have entered it. Once the door has closed upon you, you will press the button for your desired destination, and with any luck the lights will stay on. The lift however will not be for moving. Having capriciously moved when you never asked it to, it is now in 'stay put mode'. This is where the key comes in. You need the reactions of a Formula One driver to overcome the problem. Very cautiously insert your key. You may have to wriggle it around a little but do not turn it. There is some intricate relationship, known only to lift engineers, that connects key-in-keyhole to lift movement. At some stage, just when you assume that nothing is going to happen, the lift will lurch downwards. Now you act! If you do not whip the key out in a millisecond or two your grasp upon it will be lost, you will be whisked inexorably downwards at some speed whilst the still-projecting key will be macerated by the top bar of the lift as it passes to the next floor.

I would not like to leave the impression that no lifts have inner doors. Some do. Indeed, both inner and outer doors come in the most wonderful variety of styles, some striving for elegance, some for functionality, whilst others simply want to impress. There are hidden gems amongst the 1950's apartment blocks of Thessaloniki, places where even the most intrepid would never to venture without local knowledge and, for preference, a local guide. Thus I found myself being led by my friend, Christina, into a slightly shabby apartment block somewhere a few blocks northwest of Kamara. The lift was in its usual secluded place, at the very back of the foyer and set at right angles to the incoming visitor, just in case it could be discovered too easily.

Christina opened the white metal lattice door of what might have, in different circumstances, been a secure dog kennel, or perhaps a barrier against a ferocious animal in a zoo. Instead, it gave upon a secondary door of some beauty. It was a deep red mahogany, also boasting a metal grill, but smaller and of a much more refined design than its outer colleague.

"Ella," she said, and I went in after her.

There was barely room for the two of us in the almost pleasing interior. She shut the inner door, and suddenly my world changed. That which had been an innocuous, indeed mildly inviting structure, became a fortified jail. The confined cell, the small barred window, the gloom and the lack of any form of door handle left me in little doubt that we were now imprisoned

I nodded rather feebly, and not without trepidation, at Christina's suggestion that I might like to experience the workings of this lift. She punched the fourth button of an exquisitely small panel. I wedged myself into the back left hand corner of the 'asansor' expecting brutal treatment from this prison of the 1950's. The lift however rose silently and obediently to the third floor.

I glanced at my guide. From what I could see in the dim light she had a faraway look in her eyes. She was once again that imaginative five-year old experiencing the trauma of a solitary journey with but little hope of escape. But these were the horrors of yesteryear. Today she hit the lowest button and without demure this ancient cab returned us to street level and to some degree of equanimity.

Clearly the Greek lift is not a vehicle suitable for moving house. Its size, weight restriction and general attitude to working order make it impractical when it comes to shifting pianos, sideboards and the like. Such furniture moving is accomplished by the deployment of an almost infinitely extendable elevator platform that rises from a lorry parked in the road down below. Such simplicity, speed and safety would be more than satisfactory were these attributes to be found in the design and operation of the internal lift.

22

Greek Pavements

Negotiating a Greek pavement is not for the unwary. Those of us who hail from Northern Europe come from lands where pavements are quiet, orderly places where the pedestrian can stroll, gently, and unmolested. Not so in Greece!

It is all too easy to be lulled by English experience into thinking that pavements are safe places to walk. Do not be so complacent! Here the pavement is an extension both of the road and the bordering shops, but perhaps most of all the Greek character! Negotiate the crossing of any street corner and you will find yourself squeezing between crazily parked cars, but of course that is just the start! Cars and motorbikes are jammed into every conceivable stopping place leaving only the rubbish skips open to the roadway. The cars are bumper to bumper making their extraction almost impossible, as is borne out by the scratches that every Greek car has on all its four corners. Double parking is commonplace, leaving the inner cars most effectively trapped, although the more considerate of double-parkers leave mobile numbers on their windscreens.

Motorbikes have a more relaxed attitude – why even pretend that they are supposed to be confined to the road when there is a handy piece of pavement that can be utilised? Indeed this does not just apply to parking. Pavements and pedestrianized areas are 'open house' for the motorbikes that zoom along them just as happily as they negotiate wrong-way riding along one-way streets. . But on no account should you react to their presence, however fast they may be approaching you! Only the other day two motorbikes passed me in quick succession. Foolishly I attempted to dodge the first thereby very nearly causing an International Incident. But I learn fast for it was borne upon me before the swift arrival of the second that I should not stop, turn, or do anything other than keep walking. It is best to let the bikes do the dodging thing. They are Greek. They are good at it! That second one swerved competently passed me.

These pavements are not the smooth flat surfaces of home, where a slightly raised paving slab would undoubtedly be the subject of a large damages claim against the Local Council. Not only is there an unevenness due the creative Greek pave-layers having followed the contours of the land, but whole paving slabs are missing leaving gaping holes that are determined to engulf English feet. Trees have been uprooted leaving only root-holes to trap the careless. Sometimes pavements just run out – there you are walking along in a happy, but cautious, manner – and you find yourself thrust into the highway as the pavement gives way to a projecting house.

Cafés spill out across the pavement leaving a narrow thoroughfare between tables, whilst shop owners sit outside their establishments at small tables taking coffee with their friends. Then there is the access to the low-level shop, this is achieved by the construction of steps from the pavement leading down to the 'Lower Ground Floor', but there are no railings around these iniquitous wells that, particularly at night, lurk gleefully for the uninitiated. Of course every couple of hundred metres, the pavement narrows drastically as plonked dead in the middle of it is – a Periptero. People ease themselves passed and continue on their way to be harassed by the pavement people - beggars and street traders.

The pavement is a place of sharing. Yes, pedestrians are tolerated, but parked cars, cafés, beggars, fast motorbikes and kiosks all have their own claims to the use of this overcrowded pathway. There is allegory here. Northern Europe with its clear, organised but 'cold bottomed' pavements; Greece with its chaotic, 'on the edge', but essentially hospitable ones. For me there is no contest!

23

The Second Dog

Perhaps we should not have been in Vrakades. Indeed the whole idea of going to Lagkada had lost much of its appeal along the rough dirt-track that had brought us this far. The road map had declined to consider it a route worthy of mention and Mr. Google had long since gone into a signal-less sulk. Let's face it my three female companions and I were lost.

Salvation appeared in the form of a stooped figure dressed entirely in black.

"Stop, Gordon," cried my Harpies, speaking as if to the victorious Banquo and Macbeth. Car widows descended and Greek pleasantries were exchanged, pleasantries that, as is the way on Ikaria, lasted some ten minutes.

"Let's go"

"Which way?" I said.

"The lady said turn left," said Rena, "then right at the second dog."

"Don't be stupid."

"No, that's what she said."

It is entirely within the realms of my knowledge of Greek for such a linguistic error to occur, but Rena and her two friends were native Greek speakers. They assured me the lady had said just that. We proceeded.

Three minutes later the car turned a sharp bend and there, much to my surprise was a dog kennel. Chained to it and lying in the shade of a nearby tree was a brown and yellow dog.

"One," said Rena, then after a moment's pause added, "I think they must use them to deter goats from wandering back down the road."

Just over a kilometre further and the car breasted a rise. There, also chained to its kennel, was a brown and white version of the same.

"Two," said Rena, "Turn right."

Goat deterrent or not this island had devised a unique form of canine signposting. But having said that these animals have to put up with much suffering. They are out in the heat of the day, usually without any shade save a rickety 'kennel' made of wood and corrugated iron. More often than not they have no water supply. They are considered as 'tools' by their owners, and like any tool it will in time break or become useless and will be thrown away – such is the fate of the 'milestone dogs' of Ikaria

*

Recently legislation has been introduced that outlaws this treatment of dogs. I fear that it may prove difficult to enforce.

24

Οxι Day

That bravely mouthed but bitter word, so sure
to conflict nations in the bitter cold,
there to redefine 'hero' and endure
the Pyrrhic victory that would soon unfold.
You gained respect, but then lost your country,
overwhelmed by a force you could not stay,
just as at long-recalled Thermopylae,
you saved honour, but could not save the day.

Now a cause for yearly pompous glory,
a sabre-rattling show in futile might.
No warning whispers 'o, memento mori'
can stifle jingoistic mental blight.

So cruelly abused, both by friend and foe,
this nation celebrates the concept: 'No'.

25

East or West?

Anna sits, as she does so often, watching her television. She sees the Sultan clad in his magnificent clothes dispensing judgement upon those being brought before him, and she holds her breath as she waits to hear the fate of the gorgeous doe-eyed beauty that prostrates herself in front of this potentate. Anna knows that this is pure escapism. It is a bid to remove herself from the harshness of her life in Piraeus. She is aware that it is but an attempt to distance herself from the cold and the starvation and the privations that the Crisis has brought upon her and her family.

It is getting dark and she gets up to light a candle. She smiles wanly at her involuntary movement towards the TV remote. There has been no electricity here this last three months. The Sultan and his retinue creep quietly back into the depths of her imagination.

Do not imagine that this situation is rare in the Greece of today. But what is perhaps interesting is that Anna's imagination takes her to Turkish television and the programmes she used to watch when she had electricity. This is the case for the majority of Greek people. Their favourite 'soaps' are Turkish, with Greek subtitles. But why should this be?

Well perhaps the strangest thing about that question is that we should have to ask it. For it is a Western European question, one that comes from our long-held expectations of Modern Greece – and how misguided we are in those expectations. There are two Western European views of Greece, firstly the 'Classical' one and secondly the 'Sun/Sea/Sand/Sex' one, and these two overlap slightly.

The Classical view is that which the educated classes of the Western world have propounded for the past three centuries or more. That there is a country called Greece which holds all the attributes of Ancient Greece – the wonderful culture that gave us our own civilization. The Golden Age that offered us the kernel of true democracy, architecture, philosophy, mathematics, and so much more. Generations of Westerners have been schooled in the Classics, and have learned to read Ancient Greek. We thus have philhellenism in our hearts.

This was no mere scholarly feeling, for such was the Western fixation on the idea of a revival of (Ancient) Greece that the Great Powers of the time – England, France and Russia took it upon themselves in the mid nineteenth century to help those that occupied much what is now southern Greece defeat the Ottoman Empire and form the Modern Greece of today.

But what was this Greece? Where did it come from? An Englishman's grasp of history beyond the shores of our own islands is a woeful indictment of our educational system.

There is perhaps a general awareness of the Roman Empire and a sort of vague recollection that is was 'over-run by Barbarians' in about 450AD. Whilst this is, to an extent, true it is only so of the western portion of the Roman Empire. That there was a division of the Roman Empire in 395 AD has escaped most of us, although it led to perhaps the most successful and influential Empire of all time and the one that kept the candle of civilized values burning for the thousand years that it took before Western Europe picked up that baton.

The Byzantine Empire was, initially at least, Roman, but its official language, and that of most of its vast population, was Greek. Not Ancient Greek, but something more akin to the Greek that is spoken today. The richness of its culture owes more to the influences of the East than those of the West for its capital Byzantium, later Constantinople, now Istanbul, stood at the crossroads of civilizations and its influence extended to all its peoples, including the area of land we now know as Greece.

The Ottoman Empire finally defeated Byzantium and took Constantinople in 1453 It was a regime inspired by and sustained by Islam. But it was not at all zealous in insisting that its population should subscribe to that religion. Its success was in no small part due to this tolerance and the autonomy it offered to individual states and peoples – provided they paid their taxes, thus they encouraged the immigration of Jews from Spain to Thessaloniki. But again the culture of this new regime was even more Eastern than Byzantium, indeed the newly emerging Western culture saw the Ottomans as their enemy.

So from 395 AD to 1830 the land that we now call Greece was influenced almost entirely by eastern culture. Furthermore the Great Schism of the Christian Church in 1054 formalised the position of Greek Orthodoxy as quite distinct from Roman Catholicism, thus confirming Greece's separation from the West

The romantic notion of Ancient Greece as propounded by Lord Byron and his fellows led to a construct, a state founded upon an almost mythical idealism, as exemplified by the German promotion of Athens, then little more than a village, to be the capital of Modern Greece. The expansion of the country in 1912 to include what is now northern Greece added a population with an even more Eastwards orientation.

The 'Sun/Sand/Sea/Sex' view is simpler than the Classical one. This country of less than 12 million people is host to some 17 million tourists every year. For five decades or more western Europeans have flocked to the beaches, especially the island beaches, of Greece. They arrive by plane. It is no more than a three-hour journey, and they stay in resorts that ooze with western trappings. When these holidaymakers return with their suntans and tales of this gorgeous land they have not even scratched the surface of the culture. To them it is an adventure to a country where the road signs are written in a funny script. Apart from that it is as western as their own country, and most regard Greece as being much the same as Italy, but a 'bit further along'. Such is the arrogance of the West that we do not listen, we do not see, and above all we do not understand that which we experience.

Both these views combine to provide the illusion that Greece is a Western European country. And the situation is reinforced because the 'elite' of Greece, those with money and/or political power are educated in the West. Most well-to-do Greeks have spent time in Western Europe or the States, either as students or working as professional or business practitioners. And they, most particularly the politicians, have propelled Greece unrelentingly Westwards. Venizelos did so in the early C20th, and Karamanlis followed his example in determining that Greece should join the European Union (then very much a Western club) which it did, as the community's 10th Member in 1981. Membership of NATO (1952) and Greece's inclusion in the Eurozone (2001) has placed the country firmly within the Western fold.

And yet Anna looks East for her entertainment, for such is her culture, a culture that has been ingrained into the population throughout the best part of two millennia. Just over a hundred years ago this city of Thessaloniki, from whence I am writing this, was Ottoman. Whilst the politicians of Greece and Western Europe are as one in seeing Greece as a Western country, her population hold within their hearts a more Eastern, or at least Balkan, culture. It is a largely unrecognised dichotomy.

26

Lazy Greeks

Eva sits, in the nonchalant way of cats the world over, upon the grey, plastic topped, inspection table giving scant attention to the white-coated Vasiliki as she concludes her careful diagnosis. Two pills twice a day for a week and this young tan and white feline should make a full recovery. Of course the pills are expensive. Everything is expensive here.

Nothing out of the ordinary one would imagine, except we are in a run-down suburb of Thessaloniki and Eleni, Eva's owner, has brought her to the animal surgery at 8.30 on a Saturday evening. No, this is not a special appointment. Vets work long hours here in Greece. They have to. They need to make a living.

Eleni also works long hours. She and forty colleagues from schools around Thessaloniki have just returned from a coach trip to Mount Olympus where they have been busy all day collecting information that will help them to plan future lessons and perhaps, if they can manage the funding, allow them to take students on field visits. They, and hundreds of other 'lazy' teachers like them throughout this maligned country give up every other term-time Saturday to do this, not just without pay, but funding it themselves with a hard-earned €20 for the hire of the coach and refreshments. And if that is not enough many of them will be in school tomorrow, on Sunday, working with their kids on cleaning up the neighbourhood or involving them in conservation tasks designed to improve the tatty environment of this run-down area,

Why do they do this? They do it because they care. They, and their pupils know that the only way out of the grinding poverty and the muddle of politics and economics that has beset them of late is through education. These teachers are determined that if their young charges want to learn then no effort will be spared to achieve this. If this means using their own time and money, then so be it, they are teachers and they have a responsibility to the young. It is a spirit that is hard to find in more affluent societies.

Eleni works seven days a week. She does so selflessly and without expectation of much reward, which is just as well! Surely she should obtain some recompense for the long hours of her own time that she so readily offers to 'the State'? She receives no such 'overtime', instead, as a direct result of the intervention of 'The Troika' she has been battered by pay-cuts that would be unthinkable in the UK. In 2010 she was earning €1,400 per month, this being about half that earned by her UK equivalent, but if sensibly managed it was enough for a reasonable lifestyle. Two years and three pay-cuts later she now earns just €900 per month, a reduction of over one third, and the pension that she had banked on to see her through her declining years is now almost worthless. As a government employee she has no chance of escaping payroll taxation whilst the property taxes (broadly equivalent to Rates in the UK) that she must pay are collected through her electricity bill. No payment means no electricity. In this harsh world of Greece candlelight is now a tough reality.

Eleni is not alone. Throughout this country people are working long hours, most days of the week and for little financial reward. Ask your hotel receptionist how many days she works. Talk to your taxi driver. Chat to anyone you sit next to on the Metro or the bus. Nearly everyone speaks English and will readily discuss with you the problems that beset their country and themselves. If they are 'fortunate enough' to have a job in this land of gross unemployment they will be working long hours and they will be anything but the typified 'Lazy Greek'.

Yet, this is a people who know that however harsh life is, however tough the conditions of the moment, there should be friendship and laughter and good conversation. So after nine or ten o'clock in the evening the bars and the tavernas fill up, not with the riotous drinking louts of modern English culture, but with friends enjoying an evening together, appreciating each other's company, putting the world to rights. And whilst they are of course the masters of making just one beer, or one small cup of coffee last the whole evening, not one bar owner minds that in the least. There is an understanding here an empathy with the plight of one's fellow travellers in this land of ruined hopes.

We are the lazy ones, not they. Laziness is what we come to Greece to indulge ourselves in. There is a leaden irony in the way in which we project our own sloth upon these Greek people. The Brits and the Germans and the Americans come to Greece in their thousands, seeking a week or two of 'Island Living' – by which we mean slobbing around on the beach and in the resorts - amusing ourselves in every possible way whilst at the same time criticising those less fortunate than us. If we northern Europeans, were prepared to heave ourselves out of our sun-loungers for a moment or two and look inland, away from the sandy beaches and this inviting sea we might just change our minds about Greeks being 'lazy'. The scales might just fall from our eyes as we witness a whole country that is desperately and blindly trying to pay its way yet sinking deeper and deeper into debt

The popular myth of Greece being but a feckless nation was created by, and is now fed by, the media who would have it that Greeks do little work, pay no taxes, have large pensions and retire at fifty! This is so far from the truth. This proud, diligent and hospitable nation has been tarred with such a cruel brush. Of course, here in Greece, some people do 'retire' at fifty, but so do many of the men and women who comprise our armed forces here in the UK. The difference is that in the UK they receive a reasonable pension whilst in Greece the pension received by public servants is risible. Furthermore here in Greece the pension serves in lieu of any proper Social Security. The fifty-something pensioner, no doubt laid off from their former job, will now support unemployed children and grandchildren from their much reduced early 'pension'.

It is true that the lifestyle of Greeks, along with the people of other southern European countries, seems relaxed to our pitiless northern eyes. But the ability to relax, not to mop one's fevered brow every time a problem presents itself, does not mean that those who appear so laid back are not working. Our 'protestant work ethic' would seem to be not just a matter of hard work – but also an assurance that hard work is being carried out. To be seen to be working hard is everything. I can recall a colleague who told his wife that he 'had' to work every Sunday morning, then made himself a cup of coffee at the office and read the Sunday Times. In Greece no such weird psychological hang-ups exist, there is a different, more honest attitude. If there is a need to work then work must be done, if not – then to hell with how the world will label us – we are going out to play!

27

Nil Desperandum

I suppose it might not have been the very best day to go out and buy curtains. But although overcast it was not raining in Thessaloniki, and my growing realization of the need for privacy in my new apartment had made imperative a visit to the Martiou Laiki on this particular Saturday in search of net white drapery.

I researched my options with Mr. Google and between us we decided that a number 3 or 39 bus should do very nicely. It is but a short walk to the Μητροπολη stop but as usual I had to hurry to be sure of catching a bus in time to meet my friend Chrysoula at Martiou. As I approached the stop I was struck by the singular lack of people waiting. The board confirmed my fears, no buses today. I supposed that the drivers had, once again, not been paid and so were out on strike. There was nothing for it but to take a taxi.

As we sped towards the White Tower I asked my driver about the bus strike.

"Oh no," he said, "It's not a strike, it is the opening of the Trade Fair. "Samaras is coming to do the honours and every year he uses this occasion to make a speech about the economy."

"So why the lack of buses?" I asked.

"Because of the protests. Every year it happens. The politicians give us their version of the truth, and we, as I think you English would say, blow a raspberry' at them."

I was struck as much by my driver's grasp of colloquial English as I was of the need to close off roads and stop public transport just because the Prime Minister was about to make a speech.

Later that afternoon things became rather clearer. Police were out in numbers that would gladden the heart of any second division football club and these white-helmeted human shields were backed up by the military, indeed I was nearly overwhelmed by a detachment of soldiers who were running (yes running!) down Alexandrou Svolou.

Could this really be democracy. These twin bastions of law enforcement were equipped with what looked to my untutored eye like assault rifles, whilst above our heads whirled two or three 'spotter' helicopters. Admittedly the chanting of the protesters was vociferous, and their numbers were certainly formidable, but Greece is a democracy. It did not much look that way on Saturday afternoon.

Only two days before I had watched a film showing harrowing account of the Greek Civil War. It is a sad reflection on the rudimentary knowledge of European history that exists within the British Isles that a substantial majority of my compatriots are totally unaware of this terrible event when Greek fought Greek and over 70,000 people were slain. And for what? The outcome was inevitable. Once the Americans took over from the British the resources that became available to the Nationalists were vast, given in the name of the 'global fight against communism'. Whilst at the same time Stalin had already agreed with the Western Powers that Greece should stay within their sphere of influence.

Nevertheless Greek fought Greek. Families were torn apart and atrocities committed by both sides. Villages were decimated and the economy ground to a halt, and all this at a time when most of Europe was at last managing to pull itself together after the Second World War.

The end came with some of the remnants of the Partisans fleeing across Greece's northern borders whilst the remainder faced imprisonment, torture and death. And the world knew nothing about this, or wanted not to. There followed a period of right-wing government that, when challenged, produced the Junta of the 1960's.

So any true sense of democratic government in Greece can only be about 40 years old, and that is such a short time in comparison with the UK, where we had our Civil War over 400 years ago! When you look at it like that it is amazing that Greece is as civilized a democracy as it is. In the past politicians have been assassinated in Thessaloniki and it is surely sensible that their successors should be properly protected. Yes they are corrupt, but that is just a matter of degree. Yes they peddle lies, but again you show me a country where every politician tells the truth on all occasions.

So Greece, I welcome the maturity of your democracy that allows your Prime Minister to travel where he will to make speeches, and allows noisy but well-intentioned protests to take place on your streets. I welcome the fact that your leaders think it worth their while to 'massage the truth' a little to impress their electorate. I welcome your incredible ability to overcome those awful events that are still in living memory. I know that things are not perfect, but look back and remember just how grim they were. Yes there are threats to be overcome in the future, but I firmly believe that Greece will manage these in a mature way.

As the last few protesters straggled down Tsimiski I was pleased to see from my balcony that the small police unit that had been sheltering from the light drizzle under a shop canopy in Proxenou Koromilla was now leaving. That the helicopters had returned to their base, and that no one had been hurt, let alone killed. In short I, a foreigner, am proud of the evolution of the democratic process that is now extant in Greece, despite all that has been suffered by the people of this wonderful country.

Oh yes, and the new curtains look really good!

28

Philhellenes

On the Twenty Third of April those of my friends in Greece called Γεώργιος will be celebrating their name day, whilst in England the red and white cross will fly from churches and public buildings to honour the patron saint of that land. The reason for both these events is the ascribed martyrdom on 23rd April 303 AD of a Roman tribune, born to a Greek father. St George was executed in Nicomedia for failing to renounce his Christian faith.

One hundred years ago, on exactly the same date an English naval lieutenant died aboard a French warship and was buried, in great haste, in a secluded bay on the island of Skyros. He was Rupert Brooke, one of England's finest war poets, who was on his way to take part in the invasion of Gallipoli. In 2015 a small celebration was held on Skyros on 23rd April in memory of this Englishman buried on Greek soil. 'The Soldier', probably his best-known poem, is a sonnet peculiarly apposite to the occasion of his death. The opening lines are:

If I should die, think only this of me:

> *That there's some corner of a foreign field*
> *That is for ever England. There shall be*
> *In that rich earth a richer dust concealed;*

Brooke had travelled extensively prior to the 1914-18 war but despite his final resting place it appears that he never set foot upon Greek soil until shortly before his death. Brooke was an idealist but did not profess a particular interest in Greece, and it is thus by strange fortune that his mortal remains should be interred upon an island in Greece whilst those of ardent philhellenes have been returned to their own country. Perhaps the most notable English example of this is that of Lord Byron who died at Messalonghi in 1824 and whose body was repatriated to England. Mind you there is an apocryphal story that his heart was never returned but was buried in the town. I like that. Byron's heart surely never left his beloved Greece.

Writing of such things leads me to ponder upon this strange affection for Greece that lies within English hearts. Like most Western nations the English pay, or at least paid, educational homage to Classical Greece, and Englishmen, certainly of my generation, are well aware of its ancient history. We learned of the competing Nation States, we were carried away by the Spartan courage at Thermopylae, and enjoyed the wonderful tales of Greek mythology. This immersion in Classical Greece at least partly explains the philhellenism of the C.19th for it became an idealistic principle that a New Greece should be constructed on the hallowed soil of its Classical forebear.

In practice Modern Greece is far from a clone of that which existed over two millennia ago. This land which is now Modern Greece has been subjected to Roman, Byzantine and Ottoman rule whilst its population has evolved from a strong mix of peoples from other areas in the Balkans and from Asia Minor. Yet there are those of my countrymen who have fallen in love with this new Greece, Durrell and Leigh Fermor to name but two (I am claiming them although one was born in India and the other was Irish!), although neither of them died or was buried in Greece.

Why this should be is something insubstantial, a will-o-the-wisp. I feel it within myself, this affinity with a country that is in many ways the antithesis of that where I was born and bred. There is a Germanic streak within the British. We like things to be 'in order'. We stick rigidly to the 'rule of law'. We have a strong sense of civic responsibility. We also have an expectation of a 'life plan' that involves: Birth, School, University, Job, Marriage, Children, Seniority, Retirement, Death. If at any stage before the last we wish to break out of this continuum then it seems appropriate to remove oneself to a country where life is lived in a rather more disorganized, and much more endearing manner.

However at a time when Greece desperately needs technologists and entrepreneurs we, the dreaming escapee idealists from Northern Europe, are hardly the most appropriate imports to give this country the structural stability that it so desperately needs. Our contributions, if any, will inevitably be to add just a smattering to the rich diversity of Greek culture through art and writing and music and other 'left brain' activities.

Rupert Brooke was fighting in what was at that stage an idealistic war. Prior to that he had travelled much of the world, and had nearly settled on a Pacific island. He, and indeed the philhellenes, were perhaps able to take themselves and their lives to a foreign land because they carried within them the 'comfort blanket' of an idealized homeland. Perhaps I too do just that. Brooke expressed it so well in his humerous if slightly maudlin poem 'The Old Vicarage, Granchester', the last few lines of which are:

Say, is there Beauty yet to find?
And Certainty? and Quiet kind?
Deep meadows yet, for to forget
The lies, and truths, and pain?... oh! yet
Stands the Church clock at ten to three?
And is there honey still for tea?

Within the Western world there is a clear admission that we owe so much to Greece for giving us the model for democracy, complete with architecture, philosophy, theatre and the other facets of civilized society. However there lies a further truth in that Modern Greece has something just as important to offer – but unless you feel it within your psyche, you can never know it.

29

The Way Ahead

She lay, comfortable as you like, basking in the heat of the morning, and she was not moving for anyone. Strange, perhaps, that she should choose the tarmac. One would imagine that the dusty grass in the cooling shade of the nearby Holme Oak might have provided a more suitable, indeed quite desirable resting place for a dog. But no, this lactating bitch had determined that the highway was hers. Gingerly I navigated the small hire car around this immovable object and headed for Ormylia.

Greek roads, indeed Greek driving, has an element of the undiscovered, the unexpected, and the unexplainable, as do direction signs in Greece. The charming little town of Ormylia lies between the tourist hotpots of coastal Halkidiki, and the wilder uplands to the North. It is a sleepy place of lightly frequented taverna and flower-draped dwellings, of wide highways and narrow cobbled streets – and no road signs! One wonders if the municipality sets out with the purpose of confusing the visiting motorist, whether funds ran out at the crucial juncture, or if no one in the town quite realized that the world was not totally familiar with how to navigate from Ormylia to Polygyros.

I suppose the critical point in my navigation came when the width of tarmac that purported to be the main highway split into a one-way system. In itself this would seem to pose no particular problem, save for the lack of signs, or even a vague visual hint of how to rejoin the opposing carriageway. Men don't ask for directions, they clearly learned this when tracking Sabre Toothed Tigers and have failed to unlearn it in the succeeding millennia. Women have no such scruples. I was driving so stopping was out of the question, whatever Maria thought. Anyway there was no one to ask. Ormylia had gone to sleep.

We cruised, gently at first around this undulating little maze. Occasionally a wider road would be reached.

"This is it, this is a great road, bound to be the one for Polygyros," I would say.

Moments later it had petered out into a single-track cobbled street betwixt whitewashed houses with flowers cascading down their walls. Maria's amusement grew as my efforts to find the route became increasingly desperate.

"What are you laughing at?"

"You! Your optimism is so totally misplaced."

"Better to travel hopefully than never to travel at all!"

This cliché no doubt brought us the fortune it deserved, for we rounded an exceedingly tight corner, narrowly avoiding scraping the car on the wall of a house that, not unlike that dog, considered that it could appropriate the highway. And there in front of us was the start of the one-way system. We had achieved a very respectable circuit of Ormylia. Clearly what we needed was human aid. Thankfully this appeared in the form of a bronzed Adonis, naked to the waist and heaving sacks out of his truck in the mid-day heat. Maria leaped from the car with startling alacrity, not to say indecent haste, to accost this handsome male.

There are clear advantages in travelling with a native speaker of the language. My grasp of the Greek language is rudimentary. I realize that words are long, and that phrases are extended, and that Greeks like to talk, but this simple request for directions seemed to involve just a slightly excessive amount of body language and an inordinate amount of time. Minutes passed. With much bidding of farewells and "Yasases" my friend slipped back into the passenger seat.

"Turn left at the T junction, Gordon, then right at the Nursery School"

"Is that all he said?"

"Gordon, this is Greece."

I did as I had been bid. The right turn saw us embark upon a very narrow tarmac road with no road signs whatsoever. Within half a kilometre this humble road had deteriorated into a dirt track. Ormylia was not going to go soft on us now. Within half a kilometre this humble road deteriorated into a dirt track.

"Not sure about this," I said. wondering where it might prove possible to make a three-point turn.

Maria looked at me in a pitying manner. Clearly I was not a connoisseur of the Greek road system.

The track got worse, much worse. We arrived at a machinery graveyard. where ancient bulldozers surrounded us in a bizarre mechanical tableau. I fought to maintain forward momentum as I steered my way frantically through the rutted wasteland.

"Autocross," I said.

"Is it?"

"No, not the car, well it may be cross but that is not what I was saying,"

"Sometimes, Gordon, you speak gibberish."

I was surprised at Maria's grasp of colloquial English as I explained the rudiments of Autocross to her. Then, without any sort of warning, we rounded a final heap of waste and were travelling on brand new, smooth, wide tarmacadam. Ahead of us stretched a beautifully constructed highway that gave the lie to all those potholes and encroaching verges that had taxed reactions and anticipation since we had left Thessaloniki.

This virgin roadway may have been wonderful, but any form of sign tended to be deceptive, non-existent, or wiped out by graffiti, but at their junction with the main road they give little hint their status. It was thus more by good luck that any sort of clear planning that we found what appeared to be an exceedingly small byway which duly blossomed forth into the mountain road to Taxiarchis. The road ushered us up the hillside and into the lush green of the forest.

In Greece there is always a degree of uncertainty about arriving at one's destination, at least on time. However, as Cavafy so exquisitely pointed out, it is the journey to that destination that counts, both physically and metaphorically. Thus it is that I have kind feelings towards Ormylia, for it gave us an amusing half hour, and made me realize that Time and Place and Direction are, in this country, something of a confused continuum!

30

Without and Within

So, why do I bump into people? I don't mean that I keep meeting people that I know, in fact on the contrary I keep colliding with strangers, or they stagger into me. The vast majority of these unwanted, and unwarranted, encounters occur on Greek pavements. The pavement, as I have described elsewhere, is a shared forum that offers scant passage to the pedestrian, however there is an aspect of pavement-culture that has gone, as far as I am aware, unremarked and unrecorded.

Let me explain. You can be walking along, quietly and sensibly without changing your speed or direction, when one or two people emerge from a doorway or shop and without looking, let alone pausing, cut straight across you. No sense of priority of passage is recognised, nor is any thought given to the effect their peremptory progress might have upon the unwary other users of the same space. There is just a decisive, unthinking, and unheeding emergence.

Then there is the 'greeting group'. This phenomenon involves a minimum of two people, and no recorded maximum.

Let us assume that two couples are approaching each other along the pavement from opposite directions. They know each other and are pleased to meet again (be that since yesterday or last year). Oblivious to other passers-by they stop bang slap in the middle of the thoroughfare and go through the hugging, kissing, handshaking and vociferous welcoming routine – which can last for several minutes. Not one thought is given by any of those involved to the fact that they have effectively blocked the pavement thereby forcing old ladies, the physically challenged, and stray dogs to take avoiding action by diverting to the road.

This, as I am so often wont to say, does not happen in England. Yes, of course there is the occasional mix-up where people have to sharply avoid each other, but when this occurs the apologies are profuse. Indeed it is part of our strange etiquette that the person who is wronged (bumped into) should apologise, just as much as the perpetrator. It is a moot point as to whether such behaviour of the English is politeness or hypocrisy.

Much the same situation occurs when driving. I actually think that Greek drivers are amongst the best in the world in that their reactions are fantastic and, on the whole, their judgement of speed and position is faultless. That is not to say that the experience of being driven through a large town, especially Athens, by a 'good' Greek driver is not a terrifying ordeal. 'Good' in the context that I have used it does not mean cautious, safe, or even legal. If you have the courage to keep your eyes open you will see, however, that cars cutting in front of others, changing lanes and emerging from side streets, do so without a wave of invitation from the inconvenienced, and certainly without a hand raised in grateful acknowledgement by the interloper. Again such behaviour is totally unacceptable in England. Perhaps we are not so tolerant of cars cutting in front of us, and rely more upon an open-handed gesture or flash of the lights before we carry out such a manoeuvre., however it is, without doubt, an essential part of such a scenario that the 'kindness' is rewarded with a wave of thanks.

So is this all just a matter of politeness? I am not sure. I am however certain that it exemplifies a deep cultural divide between our two countries. It depicts the difference between a society where civic responsibility is of prime importance, as opposed to a regime where what really matters is the close interaction between friends and family. In England we have had many centuries of relatively stable government during which we have learned that it is to the advantage of the individual to co-operate with systems and strangers. By so doing everyone within a society is advantaged. Such responsibility extends beyond 'civilised' behaviour to other civic responsibilities such as the payment of taxes and the maintenance of the 'shared environment'.

The cultural heritage of Greece is very different. During the centuries of Ottoman rule it was essential to survival that the family/village unit protected its members against the State. The payment of tax, be that upon produce or upon land, was to be avoided by all means possible – and that of course included bribing those responsible for the collection of such. The same morality (if it can be so considered) extended to all aspects of life. It was necessary to duck, dive, weave, and bribe your way through life in order to survive within the system.

This survival technique has extended into the short history of the modern Greek state. We northern Europeans may be a trifle reluctant to pay our taxes but we do so, and by and large, can be trusted to fill in our tax returns in an honest manner. In Greece there is the need for an enormous labyrinthine bureaucracy to achieve something like the same end. It would be ludicrous to 'trust' a Greek taxpayer to do anything other than ensure that by fair means or more questionable practices nothing but the most miniscule part of his income falls into the hands of the State.

Consider also the home and its demesne. Both the Greek and the English care for the area within their 'garden wall' providing, as best they can, a pleasing aspect for themselves and their family. The Englishman however will most likely extend this to the immediate periphery of his 'plot', mowing the grass verge in front of his house and removing any rubbish, tree branches and other unsightly elements therefrom. Furthermore he may well also take an interest in his village, or immediate neighbourhood, lobbying the parish or town council on environmental matters and perhaps even joining a local conservation group that carries out regular 'litter sweeps' and/or tree planting.

Not so the Greek. As he steps, or more likely drives, across his threshold - from the land that he owns to the 'outside world' all concept of care and nurture deserts him. The road may be potholed, there will most likely be litter and stray bits of vegetation, the area will at best look a little scruffy, at worst it will be like a bomb-site. But he does not care; it is most certainly not his responsibility.

This differing cultural heritage is the reason for such diverse behaviour. To the Greek everything 'within' his physical and emotional boundaries are his to protect and foster. This includes house, his garden, his car – and more importantly his immediate family, his friends, and his neighbours. Beyond this is 'outside' and is certainly to be disregarded, possibly treated as hostile. Centuries of experience have proven that 'bad things' come from outside the immediate neighbourhood, from outside the close-knit community.

On the contrary the Englishman has a poorly developed realisation of 'within' and 'without'. Certainly there is a vague notion of 'them' – this being the concept of some distant and uninterested authority, but the corresponding 'us' is considerably more global than the Greek 'within'.

These are different cultures. Neither is 'correct' although each will be the butt of the other's jokes and possibly even distain. That which is politeness to the one is insincerity to the other, and that which is protective to the other is insular to the one. How sad it would be if there was homogeneity, for with the adoption of such dies the characteristic of nations.

31

Take Heed

An eerie half-forgotten sound
Across this southern sea,
A tramping sound, a trampling sound,
A sound to worry the free.
The nation-states of Europe
For ten years managed to run
This currency, called the Euro,
Acting as if they were one.
I admit that at first I condoned it,
Thinking it would be fair
If everyone got together
Each with their own fair share.
But they forgot that, like individuals,
Those countries that became
Partners in this venture
Were never forged the same.
Some are sycophantic
Others are much too small,

| 154 | – TAKE HEED

There are those that work the hardest,
And a few that do no work at all
The French they bluff and they posture
But hang to the tail of the Hun.
Ireland falls into recession
As Portugal's output nears none.
Spain is scuppered by housing,
Italy by Berlosconi,
BeNeLux fear they are fading
and consider the currency phoney.
Greece they so wanted to join
that they did as the Germans said
and fiddled their capital sums,
and so started off in the red.
They lived the life that they knew,
Without striving hard to achieve
Their wages, pensions, and houses.
Yes, you could call them naive.
But that is the way that they are,
Charming and friendly and Greek,
Sharing their lives and their love
A culture that's truly unique.
But up in the North it is chill,
For the German does not like to play,
But holds to his levers of power
And stashes his Euros away.
Der Fatherland cannot abide
The Portuguese, Irish and Greeks,
So it hardens its harshest demands

For the Final Solution it seeks.
And that sound that comes on the breeze?
Tis the pound of ten thousand Jackboots,
As Under der Linden is sung
With hands raised in right-hand salutes.

32

The Illusion of a Rebellion

In 2015 the people of Greece voted decisively in a referendum. What that referendum was about is, and was, a little unclear. Ostensibly it related to an EU proposal for further bailout funds in return for greater austerity, however there were those 'scaremongers' who hyped it up as a vote for staying in or leaving the Euro. In fact the EU had already withdrawn the paper that was voted on so the referendum was about that in name only. What it came down to was a feeling rather than anything else, a matter of personal and national pride amongst a people who had had enough of being ordered around by the despised Troika. The vote was really about 'are the Greek people prepared to continue to be pushed around by the EU'. The result was of course a decisive 'Oxi' (No).

The word Oxι has a huge significance in the Greek psyche. In 1940 the Greek Prime Minister, Ioannis Metaxas, refused an ultimatum from Mussolini to allow Italian forces to occupy parts of Greece. This resulted in a bitter winter war in the mountains of North West Greece and Albania, which, against all odds, was decisively won by the much smaller, and less well-equipped Greek military. To bravely say 'No' against such overwhelming superior force is a matter of much pride as Greece celebrates 'Oxi Day' on the 28th October each year.

Would it were that the events of 5th July 2015 could be reported in the same vein. The sad result was that within two weeks of the referendum the Prime Minister, Alexis Tsipras, had totally ignored the expressed wish of the people of Greece and had signed a paper agreeing to a programme of the greatest austerity. Prior to the referendum stringent capital controls had been imposed along with a strict cash withdrawal limit. In the face of threats from the EU to impose further measures that would close down the banking system Tsipras capitulated. He said 'Ναι' (Yes).

We will never know what would have happened if Tsipras had carried out the wishes of 62% of Greeks. I doubt if the EU would have forced 12 million people into starvation (mind you, historically, Germany has 'form' in so doing) and it is unlikely that Greece would have been expelled from the Euro, not least because there is no legal mechanism for so doing! However, I will not deny that the risk was great and the future looked very uncertain. But then so it did in 1940.

When Syriza made its bid for power in the election of January 2015 many Greeks whose natural constituency was well to the right of that party voted for this new left-wing consortium because it seemed to offer some hope. Hope of a change in the order of things. Hope that the corruption and nepotism of the old parties would be eliminated. Hope that austerity could be eased. And above all hope that the stagnation of the past five years could be alleviated. From the moment Tsipras signed that paper all such hope evaporated. And what was worse the national moment of renewed self-worth that had touched every Greek heart by voting Οχι had been betrayed. Politics was just 'business as usual' and it did not matter a damn which party was in power, the attitude and the result would be the same.

Thus it is that I would suggest a new date for the Greek calendar, celebrated in an appropriate fashion it will serve to remind us all of what might have been. Henceforth every 5th July should be known as "Ναι Ημέρα" – 'Yes Day'.

33

Contrasts

I boarded the 01 bus and in doing so crossed the boundary between the cossetting anonymity of Thessaloniki airport and the reality of self-reliance in this foreign land. It is no gradual transition from international traveller to resident of Greece, but a sudden change that caught me unawares and caused a draining of self-confidence as I was assailed on all sides by things strange and unexpected. But then that is why I had come here – to both bemuse and challenge the staid old Englishman that I had been, and to enjoy the opportunity of living in this ancient city of northern Greece.

I do not travel by bus much when in London, but I know enough either to equip myself with an Oyster card, or to proffer to the driver something approaching the appropriate fare for the journey. Not so here! The driver drives. He or she does not take money, nor interact with the passengers except when pressed to do so. It is more efficient this way, and the bus service in Thessaloniki is just that. No hanging about at bus stops as the driver takes money. By judicious use of mirrors and aided by efficient pneumatically operated doors the driver can clear a bus stop in seconds.

I had bought myself a monthly bus pass at the airport kiosk thus avoiding having to indulge in the fraught process of buying a ticket on the bus. This involves squeezing your way through the crowd of fellow passengers to a rather confusing machine that is intent upon gobbling all of your money without regurgitating change. Oddly to the English mind the fares are the same however far you are travelling within the city. And to avoid the greedy on-board machine you can buy a book of ten tickets for €9.00 at a Periptero. I watched my fellow passengers as they boarded and was at a loss as to why they were sticking their tickets into funny little orange boxes perched on poles inside the bus.

"You are from England?"

The girl sitting next to me must have been reading the labels stuck to my cabin case.

"That's right, but I am living in Thessaloniki now."

"Why?"

It was a reasonable question and one that I was finding it difficult to answer to myself. "I am a writer."

This seemed to satisfy her curiosity and she was clearly pleased to be able to use her excellent English. I complimented her on it and she was delighted.

"What are those orange coloured boxes for?" I said pointing to the nearest one.

"You have to validate your ticket, otherwise you could cheat the system by using it again." She explained that if I failed to perform this ritual then I would face an enormous fine if a ticket inspector should catch me. I validated my ticket.

The 01 bus acquires a mind of its own as it nears the city centre. It displays this wayward temperament by skipping first one, then several stops at a time. I needed to hop off in the centre of town somewhere near Pavlos Mela. Squeezed in as I was by fellow travellers I managed to consult the Mr Google of my iPhone, His online maps are smart enough to predict where this independently minded bus is prepared to deposit me. It was as well that I did so.

The transition from airport to bus had been a jolt to my equanimity, but it was far exceeded by the experience of alighting upon the pavement of downtown Thessaloniki. It is not the bustle or the heat or the noise, such impacts will be found in any large city. It is the contrast that is so overwhelming. A smart store displaying ladies fashions and expensive jewellery provides an astonishing backdrop to the dark-skinned cripple lying propped against the sheet-glass with his begging bowl boasting a few measly cents. It seems unusual to a western European to find lounging at strategic points large groups of policemen that dress themselves as for war; war with their own population.

It was of course my own stupidity that caused my misfortune. Happily settled in my apartment I went out the very next day to explore the city. Cafes beckoned from all sides and eventually I chose a charming one just off Dimitriou Gounari. It was a pleasant October day and I seated myself at an outside table. The waitress seemed more amused than impressed at my attempt to order in Greek, but I persevered. I had not travelled 2500km to order Greek Coffee my native tongue.

"Where are you from?" The pretty girl at the table next to me had been smiling at my stumbling linguistic efforts.

"England."

"Ah, I thought so. You did not seem to have an American accent."

We chatted for a while. She was a student and her brother was a civil engineer in London. She had never been there, but was keen to go.

"What are you doing in Thessaloniki?"

I explained that I was a writer and was gathering material for articles about Greece and the way that ordinary people were being affected by the Crisis. I extracted my card from my wallet and gave it to her, making her promise to buy my latest novel that was being published in the States.

She was a pleasant young thing, not in the least embarrassed to have started up a conversation with someone at least three times her age. Such quiet poise is, as I was to discover, an endearing characteristic of the youth of this country.

Not so endearing are the trinket sellers that persistently circulate amongst the customers of every street café. I have no idea if they actually sell anything although I did once see a rather over-eager young man buy a single red rose for his lady from a table-wandering flower seller. Today it was the turn of a seller of religious cards to harass me. These icons were held on a stick that he waved somewhat aggressively in my face.

"Oxi." I said, and then more firmly 'Oxi, Oxi", waving my arm at this dark-skinned man wearing an incongruous bobble hat.

He jumped back to avoid my gesture and in doing so dropped the cards that spilled over my table and the ground. I got to my feet so that he could more easily recover his nasty little pictures. Presumably he had had enough of the place for he gathered most of the cards and left in a hurry. Good, he was a pest.

I was enjoying myself. The city life passed me by and I just soaked up the experience of sitting in a modern vibrant city with the ruins of an ancient palace of Rome no more than ten metres from where I was sitting. People came and went, although there did not seem to be much to hurry about in their lives. I wondered how cafes managed to survive given the length of time most customers spent over a single coffee. I was the exception in that I was eating a light meal, a cheese omelette and salad.

It was time to move on. I got to my feet to pay the bill and reached for my wallet. It was not in my back pocket. I started to search other pockets, my bag, my pockets again. The wallet was not there. I knew that I had it with me as I had taken my card from it to give to the student.

The waitress came over and I explained my predicament. She called the manager. He helped me search the area and asked people at other tables if they had seen anything untoward.

A growing sense of panic was gripping me. I had my three credit cards, driving licence, a good deal of cash, international health card, English SIM for my phone, and numerous other things in my wallet.

Surely this could not have been happening to me?

It was!

The owner, Kostos, sat me down and brought me a drink.

"But I can't pay you," I whined as I counted out the €3.65 that I had in my purse. "And I cannot pay you for the meal." Kostas put his arm on my shoulder. "Don't worry, my friend, I'm so sorry it happened to you here in my café." His English was imperfect, but a good deal better than my Greek. His hospitality at this time of disaster was much unrivalled.

Pleasant people offered their advice, a doctor and her mother, a couple of 'ladies who lunch', a translator – all determined to ensure that I should cancel all my credit cards immediately. This is not easy to do when your phone has €2 left on it, your top-up cards have been stolen and you are down to your last €3.65 in cash.

Skype came to the rescue and a Skype-phone call to the UK set cancellations in motion. I had insurance for most of the cash, but in order to claim it I would have to report the theft to the Greek police. I enquired of the whereabouts of the local cop-shop and set off in search of documentation. A few minutes later I was talking to the Guardian of the Gates in his sentry box at the front entrance of the Aristotelous police station. He was an English-speaking, pleasant young man who said I needed Room 101.

Fearful of an Orwellian connection I mounted the shabby stone staircase with some trepidation. An unkempt individual was lounging in the doorway of room 100. He did not speak

English. I was not certain if he was a policeman. I speculated that he was most likely an undercover Agent dressed in a manner to infiltrate protest groups. He did not speak English.

"Portofili – err – stolen," I said

He said something in Greek about staying where I was and sauntered into Room 101. A second man, of equal sartorial elegance, was perched on the corner of a large desk talking loudly at, rather than to, what appeared to be a 'gentleman of the road'. The thought struck me that perhaps all three of them were undercover Agents. I was clearly over-dressed for the occasion.

The two policemen spoke together. They shook their heads. The second one turned to me and in broken English asked me when where and how the wallet was stolen. I explained what had happened and told him about the card seller. It was clear to me that I had failed to place the wallet securely in my pocket when I gave the girl my card and that it had fallen to the ground. Spilling the cards was a ruse to allow the perpetrator to gather up my wallet. The policeman shrugged. He had heard it all before from stupid tourists.

"How long do you stay in 'Saloniki?" He asked.

"I'm living here."

His attitude changed considerably.

And he became positively friendly when I gave my contact information as a Greek phone number. He beamed at me and asked what I was doing in Greece. I gave him my usual authorial explanation and he clapped me on the shoulder and wished me good luck.

He relayed my responses to his colleague who opened a rather dog-eared desk notebook. He drew a line under the previous entry and laboriously wrote about five lines – presumably describing my plight. He then drew a very final line under the new entry. His mate broke off from his 'examination' of the unfortunate to tell me that if they found the wallet they would phone me. Clearly they did not expect to do so. Both then shook me warmly by the hand, and wished me well. I was surprised at the kindness of my newfound friends in the police force. Hitherto I had been very wary of the Greek police. Perhaps I should remain so.

I was none too convinced that my insurance people would accept the lack of any official paperwork from the constabulary. I needed something 'official'. It was time to be 'British'. I would visit the Consulate. I knew that this was in located in Tsimiski, as part of the British Council offices. I had been there with a Greek friend of mine when I had visited Greece some three months earlier to help organise an educational exchange visit.

A balding man in his early thirties opened the door to me. He did not look pleased to see me. His English was not good.

"I have had my wallet stolen. Perhaps you can help me?"

He reached to my right and pulled out a form, small print, all in Greek. "You should fill this in and take it to the Embassy."

"But that is in Athens."

"Yes. Take it to the Embassy."

"But I cannot get there. All my money was in my wallet."

He shrugged. "This is the British Council. We do not deal with such matters."

"But you have an Honorary Consul here."

"How do you know that?"

"I have met her, she's called Maria."

"Well she's not here today."

"But if you have an Honorary Consul then this must be an Honorary Consulate."

"This is the British Council. Good day to you."

He thrust the useless form into my hands and propelled me to the door.

With just one exception every person had been so kind and helpful about my lost wallet - the café owner, the cafe customers, the police. But not the British Consulate.

I am a British citizen.

I used to be proud of that.

About The Author

Well, yes, that's me, Gordon.

What should I write about myself that could be of conceivable interest to anyone at all - whether they know me or not. I mean you have arrived here, I hope, to read some of my short stories and poems , and I don't know about you but it is sometimes a real let-down to actually meet the person whose tales you have been enjoying - an awful disappointment.

A product of my Alma Mater. Evelyn Waugh, said when asked if he were educated at Lancing College "No, I was at school there." That sums up my opinion of the place as well. I have fonder memories of my prep school, Orwell Park where a wonderful English teacher 'O-D' encouraged me to write.

My parents owned a private pack of hunting beagles, and were kind enough to appoint me as First Whip. Strange that such sport is illegal now, mind you there are an awful lot of things that are illegal in England that I find irksome - but I had better not start on that or you may be minded to report me to the Thought Police for stepping over the line.

So I could tell you that I used to fly planes, race cars and sail boats - but why on earth would you be interested in that - anyway I did none of those things particularly well. I could tell you that I was the Regional Agent for The National Trust first in North Wales and then in the Northwest of England. I could tell you that I left the NT and established and ran a successful passenger boat business on Coniston Water. All the above is desperately uninteresting unless you actually did it!

Perhaps you might like to know that for most of my life I have owned dogs - Labradors, Golden Retrievers, but most especially Flatcoated Retrievers. But that is really between me and them and probably does not say much about my character. I suppose you could be interested to know that now I spend a large part of my life in Northern Greece (Thessaloniki and Halkidiki), and still have a small cottage in Northern England.

But if I were you I would politely ignore all the foregoing and just enjoy such poems and stories as may appeal you.

The companion volume to this book is a series of poems and a few short stories that are not set in Greece. It is called 'Touching Others', its ISBN is 978-1-0686941-2-7

www.ingramcontent.com/pod-product-compliance
Lightning Source LLC
Chambersburg PA
CBHW020422010526
44118CB00010B/381